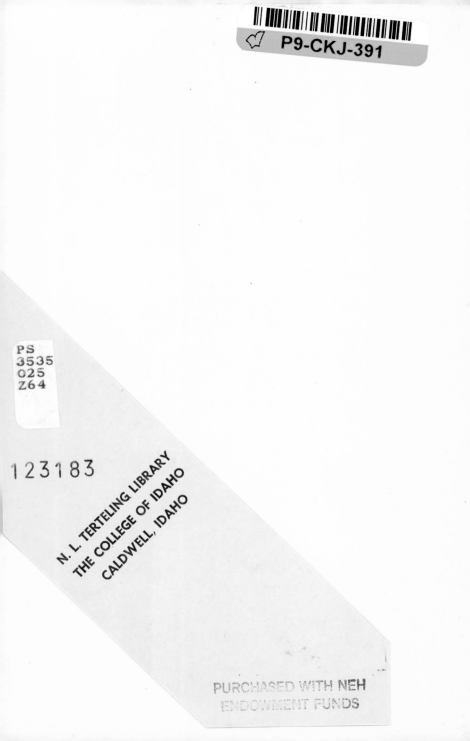

About the Author

Louis O. Coxe, Pierce Professor of English at Bowdoin College, is the author of several volumes of poetry, including *The Sea Faring, The Second Man, The Wilderness, The Middle Passage, The Last Hero,* and co-author of a dramatization of *Billy Budd.* His poems have appeared in *Poetry* Magazine, *The New Yorker,* and other leading publications.

EDWIN ARLINGTON ROBINSON

THE LIFE OF POETRY

EDWIN ARLINGTON ROBINSON

THE LIFE OF POETRY

Louis Coxe

PEGASUS   NEW YORK

Library of Congress Catalogue Card Number 69–15698

Edwin Arlington Robinson is part of a series, Pegasus American Authors, prepared under the General Editorship of
Professor Richard M. Ludwig, Princeton University.

ACKNOWLEDGMENTS

The following poems or excerpted lines from the works of Edwin
Arlington Robinson are used by permission of Charles Scribner's
Sons:

"Reuben Bright," "The Pity of the Leaves," "The Night
Before," "The Torrent," and excerpted lines from "The Clerks,"
"George Crabbe," "Luke Havergal," and "Octaves" are from
THE CHILDREN OF THE NIGHT; lines from "For a Dead Lady,"
"Two Gardens in Linndale" and "The White Lights" are from
THE TOWN DOWN THE RIVER. Copyright 1910 Charles Scribner's
Sons; renewal copyright 1935 Ruth Nivison.

Excerpted lines or entire texts of the following poems—"The
Wandering Jew," "The Man Against the Sky," "Hillcrest,"
"Captain Craig," "The Book of Annadale," "Veteran Sirens,"
"The Gift of God," "Cassandra," "Old Trails," "Tristan," and
"Isaac and Archibald"—are reprinted with permission of The
Macmillan Company from COLLECTED POEMS by Edwin
Arlington Robinson. Copyright 1915, 1916, 1920, 1927 by Edwin
Arlington Robinson. Copyright renewed 1943, 1948 by Ruth
Nivison. Copyright renewed 1955 by Ruth Nivison and Barbara
J. Holt.

In Memory of Francis Beach White

Acknowledgments

I am greatly indebted to Hermann Hagedorn's *Edwin Arlington Robinson,* which is still the indispensable biography. I have also been helped and stimulated by Chard Powers Smith's *Where the Light Falls.* The critical studies of Edwin Fussell and W. R. Robinson I have found both useful and definitive in their own special approaches. Of the many books which deal exclusively with the poetry along critical lines, I single out that by Yvor Winters as having been of considerable assistance.

Many people have helped me to a knowledge of and sympathy with Robinson's work. I acknowledge with gratitude my debts to John Richards and Willard Thorp, former teachers of mine whose literary insight and knowledge, made available to me many years ago, must have made this book inevitable, though
"The shame I win for singing is all mine."

Bowdoin College   L.C.
April 1968

Preface

To write a study of a poet does not necessarily imply that one is writing either history of ideas or history of an era, yet try as one may to remain chaste, the infection of historicism will creep in. I have no qualifications as historian of any breed or station. I have tried to see the poet whose work is the center of and reason for this book as a man, a poet and a creature of a time and place, someone like the rest of us but more so—or perhaps in some ways significantly less. Yet he came out of the past like the rest of us, too, deny it as we may. He went against his past and against his present but he never denied either the existence or the claims of what had shaped him; his own personal and familial pasts went along with new experience *pari passu;* there is as much of his own past in *Amaranth* (1935) as there is in *Captain Craig* of thirty years before—rather more in fact. The tradition he grew out of is English and New English, Romantic and Realistic. One might think of him in some ways as a perfect emanation of the Emersonian ambience. He combined, racially, two old strains, Anglo-Saxon and Scotch-Irish. And he grew up in a town of moderate size for that time and region—not a village nor a city but a rather busy, raw and ugly town very much like hundreds throughout New England. Most of all, perhaps, he was born and lived between worlds.

Edwin Arlington Robinson came to maturity—and we might take the date of his first book as index—in 1896. At that time the *Century* magazine was publishing such poets as Clinton Scollard, Curtis Hidden (sic) Page, S. Weir Mitchell, Theodosia Garrison, and the Canadian Charles G. D. Roberts. The *Atlantic,* which published far less poetry, included a few of the above and also John Bannister Tabb, the priest, and one John Vance Cheyney, who appears to have been a very hot property indeed for a brief period. Neither magazine published anything of any quality in poetry, nor did any other. Occasionally a name of some importance may show up, like Mitchell's, though as in his case the appearance owes more to the author's fame in another sphere than to his merit as poet or to the quality of his poem. Little magazines as we know them simply did not exist, and in fact it was the founding of *Poetry* in Chicago in 1912 that marked the beginning of a poetic renascence. If Robinson did appear in *Poetry*, he did so with poets a good deal younger. His early years he spent in the wilderness, for not only did he have no money and no influence, but he could find no publisher. Any poet can stand the neglect of patrons, foundations, publishing combines, critics and reviewers. But never to appear in print, when one is young and full of the fire and the rage— *that* Robinson like many before and since found intolerable to the extent that it hurt and hindered him. Between magazines like the *Century* and cheap journalism there was for the most part nothing at all. The mass circulation magazines which would drive the *Century* and others out of business had not yet come into being, and the few new little magazines were editorially timid and conventional. Even such English ventures as *The Yellow Book* did almost nothing in the way of introducing new poets or bringing out new and unconventional work. By the time Robinson achieved fame the whole society had undergone a kind of seismic change.

We might date that point at 1921, the year that saw the publication of the first *Collected Poems* and Robinson's first Pulitzer Prize. America had fought and won three foreign wars, had acquired an empire and a commercial, military and moral ascendancy over the world which everyone but America recognized. Robinson's New England had slipped from the control of the old to the control of the new and the great days of its industrial and commercial monopoly had passed. The New York he had lived in ceased to be home—he couldn't get used to the booming growth of the twenties; literary and artistic tastes had grown much more cosmopolitan, eclectic, almost camp as we today use the term. Never at ease in his own earliest world, Robinson was no more at ease in this new one, and his strategy, like that of most poets, was to try to "get used to not getting used," as Mann's Hans Castorp did, and to ransack his own past, his memory, for those exemplary and curious fictions which his imagination then proceeded to recreate. As poet, Robinson is very American—"home-grown" of the old sort, the whittler and the tinkerer and the teller with straight face of jokes and bawdry. But he also has that quality he ascribes to Lincoln in "The Master": that of being "ancient at his birth." When he is most himself as a poet, Robinson conveys a sense of authenticity, of plain wisdom about things that matter which only Hardy, of all the poets of the age, can rival, and even Hardy lacks Robinson's range of sympathy and vision. The poets who came after him—Frost, Stevens, Pound and Eliot—suggest the change in time and climate, not only because they come later but because they come from other areas than the northeast: Frost was, after all, born in San Francisco and his earliest images come from California; Stevens, from Reading, though he may be Pennsylvania-Dutch, really belongs nowhere, to the country of imagination; Eliot, from St. Louis, goes to the Boston and Cambridge of his forebears but will keep going east till he can rest in the England of more distant pasts; as for Pound, the Idaho holy terror with a rage for culture, his true Penelope was a museum.

Robinson for many years went from Gardiner to New York and back with stops in Boston. He later added to this itinerary Peterborough and the MacDowell Colony; he picked up that way station without a hitch. But that was it. One brief trip to England marked the extent of his travel abroad, as a short excursion into Pennsylvania marked his western limits. His intellectual and literary travels seem to have comparable bounds, and after he reached full maturity he does not seem to have read at all widely nor to have ventured into new realms of thought, at least if what we know of his reading is any index. His taste in poetry and fiction took lasting form early in his career. Never really more than conventional, that taste may be said to represent the middle culture of his time—neither highbrow nor low, but Average Educated Philistine, New England variety. He grew up in a household which contained the usual vaguely literary mother and resolutely commercial father. The latter, however, saw nothing dangerous in a bit of poetry and song around the house, so long as no one took it seriously, the business of America, as Calvin Coolidge would deathlessly put it, being business. There were parlor anthologies and William Cullen Bryant was a great favorite. Robinson later fell under the influence of Wordsworth, by his own testimony and by that of a few poems, notably "Isaac and Archibald." He specifically rejected the suggestion frequently made, that Browning influenced him. As a very young man he discovered Kipling and read him all his life—the two men died within a few months of one another. And he found pleasure in the work of Housman. Aside from these latter two, we do not find any others of whom he spoke with enthusiasm. He helped his friends who were writers, but one somehow doubts that he admired the poetry as much as he expressed loyalty. In sum, I think it safe to say that Robinson's taste, ideas and literary interests correspond closely to those of his contemporaries in any line of endeavor. He simply went directly about being a poet of a sort called "new" or "unconventional" without apparently preparing for the task by schooling himself in "original" work of the time. He did admire Meredith, who, if not original, was certainly difficult by the standards of his time, but the writers he really admired and reread and who formed his taste were the great Romantic poets, Shakespeare, Latin poetry, particularly Virgil, and nineteenth-century fiction, American, English and French. Emerson impressed him greatly, and so did Whitman for a time, not so much in the long run by their ideas or attitudes as by their force and their language and techniques. He read Hawthorne avidly, and though we cannot really tell how much of Henry James he read nor how deeply James's fiction impressed him, I think the evidence shows a reasonably direct influence.

All this demonstrates, if anything, that poetic geniuses are not necessarily of the wilder sort, that poets are as various as men in general. Just about all of them start reading very young and read what there is at hand, from the Bible to shoddy fiction, from Shakespeare to Ella Wheeler Wilcox. Robinson lived a conventional life for his first twenty years. Much wider horizons appeared when he went to Harvard, but after his return to Gardiner the world seemed to close in on him again. We can, I suppose, lament that he was not born in a better time and place, which would only show that either we don't mean anything at all or that we want a wholly different poet. The limitations in education, upbringing, taste and whatever that we note in the man and his work simply describe that man and that work, or one aspect of them; they do not explain nor present an alternative. The poetry is there, warts and all. I hope this book may help to define an approach to that poetry, thereby making it more accessible.

Contents

EDWIN
ARLINGTON
ROBINSON

THE LIFE OF POETRY

COURTESY: TIME MAGAZINE

I

Critics, Biographers
and Readers

Some poets must, from beyond the grave, beg from time to time to be delivered from their friends. A critic poets can treat after his desert, whipping and all, but friends are another matter. In the case of Robinson, we must resort to the term "poetry lovers" if only because those who wrote about him so often seem to merit that more than equivocal term. Something like "bird watcher," one suspects: people in funny hats looking at odd things at odd times. It is a term of contempt, fundamentally; neither a real critic nor a person of genuine sensibility can be said to love poetry. They dislike it too and give themselves to it wholly only when the poem itself commands. I take it that that is what the word "critic" means, in part. That Robinson should have dedicated his first book, only partly facetiously, to "any man, woman or critic who will cut the pages . . ." we can take as evidence that he knew or at any rate sensed from the start that critics are not men and women, as a rule, nor men and women critics. Like any other beginning poet, he was left to his own resources of influence, money, self-advertisement, friends and genius. Of all but the last two he was destitute, and surely we must finally agree that the very genius itself suffered from neglect and abuse. America has a certain way with its poets and novelists, killing them with either kindness or neglect of a sort so cold and all-encompassing that only the most tenacious writer can survive it. Robinson grew into a period, of our culture as we say, that must surely rank with the worst—with let us say the Second Empire of France, but immensely magnified. He barely made it and the cost was prodigious, and not to him alone.

The time was that of inchoate Chicago, of the great robber barons, many of whom today belong to our pantheon. It was the time of TR's "splendid little war," of "our little brown brothers," of those giants of literature Thomas Bailey Aldrich and F. Marion Crawford. And most important, perhaps, it was significantly for Robinson not the time of either the patron or the foundation, of the government pension or the poet-in-residence. A poet was supposed, like any entrepreneur, to get in there and fight to make his living. Of course the country had many such men of letters (as opposed to poets) to show for just such a fine capitalistic dispensation: Mark Twain, William Dean Howells—there were two American success stories for you! Small-town boys who made good, as it would seem. But what it did to them as writers was neither here nor there. They could always be like Thoreau, couldn't they?

Yet the fact is that up until our own time the finest of our poets and novelists have had to survive neglect, and of every one of these it can be said that the neglect was damaging—in some cases, irremediably so. Emerson the poet, Hawthorne, Melville, Whitman, Emily Dickinson, Robinson. Of course it can always be maintained and frequently is that killing with kindness is worse; yet surely most of them might have liked a choice in the matter! Or again, don't write if you find it so hard. Who asked you to anyhow? "Who needs it," as the current phrase goes? The brutal answer is: No one. It is difficult to believe that the country would be much different if none of these writers had ever been born; art is indeed expendable which is why it is so often expended and dispensed with. Yet to some—and the point cannot be stressed enough though it is a truism—art simply gives orders and one writes against one's better judgment and reads or listens or looks at one's peril. Art is not for the idle and the leisured, though they often consume it; it exists to make life a cross for those who for whatever reason and by whatever chain of events get stuck with it. Neither MacLuhan nor NBC can help them.

Edwin Arlington Robinson had a very bad—an incurable—case. Like practically all American poets from his own forebear Anne Bradstreet to his contemporary admirer James Dickey, he was born a hick in a hick town, which is only to say that he was typical of his time and place and ancestry. From all that we can gather of his boyhood and youth, it seems that he felt "special" from the start, in the sense that he early recognized a difference between himself and the others. It never seemed to occur to him that he could fight against the difference, nor later on that he could go to work, get married, live like the "happy men that have the power to die." In later years he could only say, from time to time—on his deathbed, too, according to Chard Powers Smith—"I never could do anything except write poetry." Whether he could have or not, he didn't. Rarely has a man gone so single-mindedly to his task, and it may be that some critics and readers may say and indeed some have said, that that is exactly the trouble with Robinson's verse: it somehow escapes relevance to the deepest life, always escaping, always missing the crucial in favor of the tangential, always at the last blurring the effect rather than defining it. And there is a great deal in such strictures, as we shall see, I believe, when we examine some of the poems. Yet in a way, has the case been different with the others? Surely Robinson is closest to Hawthorne and Emerson, to the former in spirit, to the latter in his language and feel for an American style. In Hawthorne we continually sense a fine spirit, frustrated, baffled, groping; he starts forward, retreats, affirms, qualifies, retracts, leaving us "dull and baffled as before" as Phelps Putnam has it. Peering with utter intensity through his microscope, he sees (and we with him) not the microrganism he would study but his own inner eye. What Robert Lowell says in his poem "Hawthorne" has its meaning for Robinson too—and for many another American writer:

> The disturbed eyes rise
> furtive, foiled, dissatisfied
> from meditation on the true
> and insignificant.

Emerson, the New England weather—spiritual and physical—gave Robinson an appetite for transcendentals and the larger abstractions. He would have been utterly confounded by the statement of a contemporary English critic that we do not read poetry any more for truth or wisdom. For what on earth else,

would have been his reaction, along with that of the whole
New England literary pantheon, and if deep down he might
also acknowledge that certain poems have a truth and wisdom
that Poetry knows nothing of, he nonetheless could no more
stop himself from dealing with the intense inane than could
many another Romantic. And we must never forget that he is
indeed a Romantic, perhaps a Romantic Realist, but certainly
one on whom all the currents of Romantic writing converged,
from Keats to Bryant to Kipling. He desired no other fate, yet
it is ironic that, thoroughly soaked in that tradition himself, he
had to spend most of his career battling the Romantic mediocrity
that swamped the periodicals and the publishers' lists. Again
and again in his long or middle-length poems, we hear echoes,
not so much of other individual poets but of the Romantic
Style, whether transcendental, passionate or periphrastic. Pick
up any of the long poems and start counting abstract nouns!

What any reader must at least acknowledge is that there are
more Robinsons than one, as there are more Emersons, for
example. Robinson began by liking Emerson's prose, but he
ended by admiring the poetry, as notably did Robert Frost.
Both found there, I think, a kind of poetics and an approach to
subject and language which, while kin to that of Whitman,
seemed to suit them temperamentally as being both less extreme and more particular. With Robinson, the particularity is
important because in his lesser work it is absent. Not that even
in his finest work we find much concrete detail, but that the
poem is more than likely to turn on a hard, specific image, or a
cluster of images. And then, when Robinson writes really well,
he forgets generalities and largenesses in favor of these circumstances, this case. Notoriously, hard cases make bad law, and
when Robinson writes well he neither argues nor prosecutes. He
puts the case, sometimes for the drama, sometimes "for the
larger humor of it," but always for the human pity and terror.
These are the poems we read today, and which readers will go
back to for as long as readers read. Oddly, though, the poems
that made him, aside from one or two anthology pieces, were
the long or longer works such as "Ben Jonson Entertains a Man
from Stratford" and of course *Tristram*. In the latter part of
his career when asked why he didn't write short poems any

more, he said regretfully, "They don't seem to come any more." They did not. His final years were devoted to book-length poems. Why? What happened? Many critics contend with T. S. Eliot, that he is "negligible" anyhow, and just as in his lifetime he fell first under the shadow of Moody and later under that of Pound, Eliot and the new poetry, so since the thirties he has suffered from unfavorable comparisons to Frost. Such affairs are common, one might argue; literary reputations fluctuate; Robinson will be a hot property again. But the trouble is that his work has never been taken ·seriously by the literary elite of any period since he first published a book. I suppose only Melville, among American authors, ever had a comparable history. Even Robinson's *succès d'estimes* have been acknowledged chiefly in circles which no one could call pre-eminent for critical, authorial or imaginative power or reputation. Of modern literary figures with prestige and accomplishment for credentials, only one, Yvor Winters, has addressed himself to a study of Robinson's poetry— and he was promptly taken severely to task for it by no less a man than John Crowe Ransom. Once again we are back at the vexed question: Are the adverse critics right and is Robinson only a minor poet, not really worth the time and attention of those whose life is literature, or of those who can read a real poem?

I think we have to blame Robinson's friends, in the broad sense of friends: his admirers, contemporary and contemporaneous, his biographers, his memorialists and pious pilgrims. And there is a bit of a clue in his sardonic statement: "My poetry is rat poison to editors, but here and there a Philistine seems to like it." I might tentatively put forward an explanation why that was so in his time, and why what I have attempted to describe as the literary attitude to his work remains what it has been. Simply, the poems don't look enough like poetry to certain poetic folk. To others they look like the poetry they are used to. Even the obscurities are plain, as resembling Wordsworth's or even Browning's. Yet minds that never boggle at Pound's later *Cantos* simply cannot bear even the look on the page of Robinson, the while Charles Olson and William Carlos Williams are to them as rare wine. In part this is a new version of the Hucks vs. the Ahabs, Redskins vs. Palefaces, Coolies vs. Mandarins; yet it is also more than that. The effect of the new poetry of the period just before, during and after the Great War was a watershed: not only did it genuinely break up old views and styles and ways of thought, but it irreparably split the literary audience into two irreconcilable camps: the avant garde and the reactionaries. That oversimplifies but does, I think, put the case: Whereas up to that time there could be differences of opinion about poets and novelists and various works, the audience for all "good" literature was reasonably homogeneous. Then Pound said, "Make it new," and all was if not light, certainly heat. The generation of the Great War turned towards France, towards pre-Romantic literature, towards an international style, and the poetry of the immediately preceding period, the Georgian for example, seemed like pretty thin stuff by contrast. Now, today, a half century from those stirring times, we can gain a perspective—which will prove false in its turn but now serves our need.

What did the writers of that time think poetry should be? We know what their own work is like, and today we find Eliot in eclipse, Pound ignored, academicized or a mere "influence." The injustice will find correction soon, but what is Robinson's case? For the most part he exists in anthologies, each selection being chosen from a prior anthology, or so it would appear. And until recently much of his work was very nearly inaccessible in the badly printed, overpriced and obsolete *Collected Poems* (1937). The late Morton Zabel's *Selected Poems* (1965) in both paper and cloth bindings has been helpful, and there are signs that the work is beginning to reach an audience of younger readers as well as those literary men and women to whom Robinson was largely only a name. Something has changed in the poetic climate, true, but most of all, there are more and different audiences for poetry today. The Black Mountain audience, the Bob Dylan, the Poundian Diehard, the West Coast Surf and Cellar, Standard Effete, and just plain readers.

I have the suspicion that a powerful factor behind Robinson's belated success and his early eclipse has been that his poetry, as I have said in another place, keeps a prose in view. He writes a middle style in the Romantic vein, in an idiom that can comfortably accommodate to a prose syntax while it can swiftly modulate to the epigrammatic. Given the kind of Jamesian "bewildered mind" that he often likes to deal with, he will sum up an entire novella; or, with a deceptively easy gait, take us through the ironic pastoral "Isaac and Archibald," his version of "Michael," as it were. What counts here is that style both effaces itself yet is constantly present as mediator, as one who neither argues nor defends nor prosecutes, but tells and presents. Quite obviously, this Robinson was not the one the poetry lovers loved, nor the scions of the new poetry: if there was any poem of his they liked, it was "Luke Havergal" which looked as though it might have been influenced by Laforgue or somebody but of course wasn't. The poetry lovers liked the obscure, periphrastic, syntactically opaque poems because they seemed to throw shadows of meaning, deep thought, like Browning. This they often called his "philosophy," and they spilled much ink locating, exploring and explaining it. Later in this book I hope I can dispel once and for all the misconception, one which he himself specifically rejected if that means anything, that Robinson and philosophy had anything to do with one another. But be that as it may, the fact remains that both literary camps could never begin to agree as to what is or was poetry or whether a given poem was good or bad or even a pleasure to read. Without going into any reasons why, I think we can say that good bad poetry and bad good poetry sometimes last as long as good good poetry. I suppose I should say that again but I won't, since anyone who knows what the three types are needs no counsel from me or anyone else on the subject. The point is that rigidity of taste and temperament, as well as a tendency to be doctrinaire, not to say fanatical, have marked much of literature since the Great War. The French do these things better than the English and the Americans. To sum it up, the past fifty years have seen a great increase in what Santayana called, in reference to Browning, the poetry of Barbarism, and what Mr. Robert Langbaum in his *The Poetry of Experience* calls relativism. Now Robinson is above all a civilized man, a master of the middle style, a Roman, whereas poetry since 1914 has been overwhelmingly "cultured," idiosyncratic—in short, Barbaric. Robinson took the middle Romantic style and put it to uses it had not known. He made it American and he made it Realistic; and incidentally, he made it in an important sense, urban. Poetry for the most part has gone another way until just about this very moment, being largely international in style and subject, multivocal or at least in intent such, surreal or symbolist, and metropolitan rather than cosmopolitan when it has not been defensively bucolic. There is and has been no Robinsonian school, but the name of the school of Pound is legion.

Perhaps there is paradox in the notion that Robinson can be both country boy and cosmopolite, the hick and the city man. Yet most American urbanites came from the country, and to Robinson The Town Down the River was New York, not Boston, and it always remained headquarters, the place where in his middle and later career he went to get ideas and attitudes for the poetry that he would later write in Peterborough or Boston. It cannot be coincidence entirely that the first work he did in poetry was a translation of Virgil; both poets were candidly "derivative" and yet unmistakably themselves. Both were at home in town and country: *Rus in urbe, urbs in rure.* To each poet, for all he may have dealt with the forlorn and the tragic, life was good if only because it pointed beyond itself. They are poets of the civilized heart and mind, whom no one and nothing can shock, surprise or embitter. Whatever of rage and intemperance of all sorts Robinson had to listen to in his time (and it was a great deal) he could always manage "the fealty that presents / The tribute of a tempered ear / To an untempered eloquence." If Robinson is, as I think, in the process of finding at least the audience he has long deserved, the reason, or one of the reasons, may derive from just that wise, sympathetic, tolerant, but by no means indifferent steadiness of gaze that he fixes on the soul in travail.

II

Person, Place and Thing

Edwin Arlington Robinson was born in 1869 in the tiny village of Head Tide, Maine, a place that today looks totally deserted to the casual visitor. A number of prosperous out-of-staters have bought up and restored most of the fine old houses, but the house that Edward Robinson bought and where Mary Robinson bore her third son, the poet, is again in the family and stands just across the road from the Sheepscot River on the main, or only, street. In summer there are people about. The meeting house on the hill occasionally affords a fashionable wedding; it is only a question of time before a mass circulation picture magazine does up the town, the present householders and the ghost of the poet, all in color and breathless prose. The town at least can justify such treatment although it may to the sour seem to overdo it—a touch too slumbrous, quaint, idyllic? Yet it can never have been much more bustling, even in the boom post-Civil War years when Edward Robinson became the local tycoon, found the resources of Head Tide inadequate, and moved to nearby Gardiner, on the Kennebec River, a town of some forty-five hundred and in the throes of shifting from a paper, lumber, ice-cutting and shipping town to a typical New England small mill and factory center.

The Robinson family was old New England: on Mary Palmer Robinson's side the Dudleys were among her forebears, names illustrious enough for the grandest of all in Gardiner, had they known. But "they" were the real thing: Gardiners, Tudors, Hallowells and Vaughns. The Gardiner family had its enormous lands by grant from Charles II and lived in baronial splendor at "Oaklands," the Gothic Revival castle high above the Kennebec. But Mary Palmer had married a Scotch-Irish Robinson who was too newly rich to rate a title grander than the Duke of Puddledock, by which he was known locally and contemptuously, it would seem. A trivial affair, perhaps, but I think we can later see that this particular matter, of not being quite right socially, had its effect, on Robinson personally and hence on the poetry. For the Gardiners and their kin were the Big House People, lords of the shire, and even when Robinson became friends with one of the clan, John Hays Gardiner, who taught literature at Harvard and who "enjoyed poor health" as they used to say up country, he was never accepted. The great families did not "know" the Robinsons, though later, when Mrs. Henry (Laura E.) Richards took up the young poet and dragged him out into the open of her delightful house and family, at least one of the great ones became a lifelong friend. But a friend of EA, as he later liked to be called, not of any of the rest of his family.

Small wonder, in one sense. To read Hermann Hagedorn's life of Robinson is to understand what the poet meant when he wrote that he lived in hell. For a few years it must indeed have been all of that. Yet the child, the boy, the youth would seem to have had a fair enough start. Neither happy nor unhappy, we might suppose, and the poet himself wrote to Amy Lowell that he remembered, at about the age of six, rocking away in a large chair and wondering why he had been born, a question never to be answered, since Robinson would never give the Sophoclean negative nor the Whitmanic affirmative. He grew up, that we know, and grew up in a town and a busy river town at that; he was never a country boy, though he knew his way about in the woods and of course played the games and the childhood sports of such a time and place. Yet he was always "long Robinson," a touch grave and courtly in manner, perhaps comically so when he was little, never one to go in for athletics or the blood sports. The Richards family has a wonderful snapshot of him at the family camp on the Belgrade Lakes: two girls are paddling, bow and stern, a big canoe of the Indian type and in the middle bolt upright, dressed entirely in black and with a high stiff collar and what we must call a cravat, sits the Poet. Even as a youth and a young man he would make no concessions. When Mrs. Richards first heard that Gardiner had a real poet and wrote to him asking him to call, she ended her note with the tag, "Prithee, O Hermit Thrush, come out of thy thicket." Robinson answered correctly and ended his note with his tag: "I am not a Hermit Thrush." Take that. He would never be anybody's anything. He would dress and be silent and half starve in his own way, and even Theodore Roosevelt had to plead with him to be allowed to give him help.

How do we account for this strange sport in a backwater of the flush times? We don't, I expect, though there are some things we can see. In the first place, everything about Robinson's personal life as a young man, child and infant was slightly wrong—off-center, distorted. It begins with his name. He was more than a year old when one of the ladies at the summer hotel in South Harpswell where the Robinson family was summering insisted that it was high time this child with the striking eyes and complexion so like his mother's be properly named. So all the ladies wrote names on slips of paper and when one was drawn out of a hat, it was Edwin. Having gone that far, Mary Robinson finished the job by giving her son for a middle name that of the town whence the lucky lady had come: Arlington, Massachusetts. There was a kind of heartlessness about Mary Robinson that her son would touch on, fleetingly, in "For a Dead Lady." He speaks there of "the laugh that love could not forgive," and if he did in fact forgive it, he remembered just the same. He remembered later, as he must have resented at the time, the clear favoritism shown his two older brothers, Horace Dean and Herman. Dean, as the oldest was called, born in 1857, was his father's favorite, a choice the youngest boy surely understood since he looked on Dean always as the star of the family and with real hero worship. But Herman, three years older and his mother's favorite, was another matter. I think it both idle and inaccurate to worry the question of rivalry for Mum's affection; the point would seem to be, more accurately, that even as a child Robinson knew a trivial soul when he met one. Yet as a boy he must not have been much more than wistfully aware that whatever he was or might become, no one really paid or would pay much attention. They would be kind, at least in the family; they would do the right thing as they saw it, but they would never see much, as far as he was concerned. He would be on his own whatever he might do. And what he would do became more ineluctable with each year passing, only because Robinson refused to do anything that might prepare himself for a job.

Edward Robinson had it figured out: Dean would go to Bowdoin and to the Maine Medical College, Herman would go into business, and Edwin would—well, he would certainly do something after high school but it would not include going to college. But by the time Edwin was of college age, Dean, now a doctor, was demonstrating the evils of college and higher education by becoming a victim of morphine. The practice of medicine in rural Maine, in all weathers, drove him to it, to keep going. Edward had forced him into a profession to which he was fundamentally uncommitted, and after a short time as a practicing physician he came back home, to the House on Lincoln Avenue, Gardiner, to play out his particular role in the Robinsonian Tragedy.

But Herman was another matter. Some years after Herman's death, an old schoolteacher of his was asked about all the Robinson boys and he observed of Herman that he was charming, handsome, athletic, popular—and that no one ever thought he would amount to anything. For a time he very nearly fooled them. As we all know, charm and good looks will get you almost anywhere in an entrepreneurial world—as long as you are tough, hardheaded and financially shrewd. Herman was none of these. He could and did talk his father into putting his not inconsiderable fortune into western land speculation, particularly in and around the booming city of St. Louis and in Minnesota, where so many Maine folk had gone, with an eye for all that rich, flat stone-and-rock-free soil, the mills, the railroads. Herman would try to buy a piece of all that. And we know from the newspapers that for a while he was the young operator, the financial whiz kid, parlaying deals, making big ones out of little ones. And of course the bubble burst and of course Herman made the classical response and took to the bottle. He had meanwhile married Emma Shepherd, whose family was new in the district—they lived in nearby Farmingdale—and who was the most beautiful girl anywhere around. Certainly the photographs bear out the legend of that beauty. Whether or not the beauty was enough to account for the legend that all three brothers loved Emma Shepherd remains a vexed question but one persuasive enough to prompt one writer to devote a book to proving that practically all Robinson's poems are about Emma and his love for her.

But Herman did one good thing before the bubble burst: he talked his father into letting the youngest boy go to Harvard. Edward like many another small operator had never been to college and could see no use in it: it was a waste of time and money and furthermore *he* had never been to college and look at him. That is more or less the way the words and music must have gone, one imagines. And there was, unhappily, Dean to point the moral. So Robinson, two years after graduation from high school, unprepared for the regular academic course, went to Cambridge, as it turned out for two years only, as long as the money lasted. Years later when Robinson told Barrett Wendell, the Harvard eminence, that he left college after two years, the great man growled at him, "You were damned lucky." Perhaps he was. But for two years not only did he escape the hell of the House on Lincoln Avenue and of small town loneliness, but he discovered a new world.

Long before this time he had begun to write. And he was reading widely of course. As Laura E. Richards observed sadly, "We have no juvenilia," because one day when Robinson was reading some of his poems to friends in the cellar of the Lincoln Avenue house, the boys declared their disapproval of the work and into the furnace it all went. Even the class poem survives only in fragments recollected by a classmate. The earliest work that we know about, the poet himself destroyed. It could be no great loss, I think. Most of it, of necessity, must have been exercises, particularly in the intricate French forms beloved of one Alanson Tucker Schumann, a homeopathic physician and poetaster whose poems appeared in print locally from time to time, and whom Robinson actually accosted one day when he was seventeen and asked for help and guidance. The good doctor was in local literary society of the second echelon, had true competence as a versifier, and in his disinterested passion for poetry soon recognized in this awkward boy his superior in talent and taste. He took him around in Gardiner literary circles; and if we may be permitted a patronizing smile at what that society was like, it took Robinson in when he was a mere boy and it did not patronize him. He wrote steadily, not exactly secretly but as a young poet must: for himself, with only a hope of an audience to come, trying to beat out his own music and his own way of looking at the world.

The world of Gardiner was not all that provincial. In the town were a number of Big House folk who knew the great world beyond and whose sons went to Harvard. Like many New England towns whose prosperity came to some degree from shipping, Gardiner looked outward to Europe, where a number of scions of the best stock went for education and grand tours. The houses all had their Asian trophies and furnishings, loot brought back by sea captains, and of course there were the houses where the male line was gone and old maids lived alone with older servants. Unlike a middle-western town, Gardiner was near centers of commerce and civilization. There was good train service, and rivers were highways in those days; there was always a packet to Boston and a number of people came up the Kennebec for commercial reasons: the ice-cutting industry was important, as of course was pulp and paper and as shoe manu- facture would soon become. The town, which the poet would transfigure into Tilbury Town, had all those elements of decay and boom, of failure and success, of feverish activity and a kind of catatonic arrest which would seize the poet's unconscious at- tention and give him material of a richness and yet an acces- sibility that a bigger town might not have. And above all, Robinson never really belonged. Just as, socially, the Robinsons could not arrive for all they lived only a block from some of the best of Gardiner with kin and friends among the great and well-connected of the eastern seaboard, so they could not establish a sound economic basis for a more gradual ascent into the solid upper-middle class. For by the time Robinson, three months short of his twenty-second birthday, set out for Cambridge and Harvard, the time was running out for Herman and his ventures. Within a year Edward Robinson would be dead, the estate nearly gone, the family, which now included Herman's wife and their daughters, on the edge of general catastrophe.

Cambridge, Harvard and Boston saved Robinson's life. He came to these great good places a provincial naif, too near despair for so young a man, and left two years later equipped to go through the still lower circles of hell that awaited him. These we shall see in due course; now is the time to find out if we can what this young man was like, what he got from Harvard, and what in particular he brought to it and how both interacted. And first of all we should remember that he was a Maine, not a Massachusetts, boy. Not for him the rarefied company of the type Henry Adams naturally found. Though an old Yankee he was no Brahmin, had no "connections," no money, no influence. Though several years older than a beginning freshman, and though his status was that of a special student, he does not appear to have been made uneasy thereby; in fact the young men he came to know best were all of them rather special, misfits and outcasts, like Mowry Saben who was in violent rebellion against the puritanical creed of his family and in particular against the rigors of being brought up by a professor of mathematics! When Robinson met him, he met a man who had suddenly discovered freedom and who wanted to tell everyone all about it. Then there was his lifelong friend George Burnham, another New Englander, who had like Saben rebelled against his father, left home at seventeen to wander through the west and southwest working when he could, nearly starving when he couldn't and so nearly dying of cold in Wyoming that his feet had to be amputated. Here was a misfit, a tragic kind of figure after Robinson's own heart. Friends had long been his stay against despair in many ways: the Gardiner high school days were sacred in his memory chiefly because of friends and the "League of Three," a club formed for conversation, illegal smoking and the kind of mind-bending that goes on with adolescent and just post-adolescent boys. Chief of these friends— Moore, Gledhill, Smith—was the last, Harry DeForest Smith, to whom Robinson wrote, at the very least once a fortnight, during the years 1890–1900. Friends came to mean family, in a sense, but less simply they meant release from himself. And though most of the time he said little or nothing, letting the friend do the talking or keep him company in silence, all his friends who had occasion to speak of Robinson for publication attest to his remarkable capacity to convey a sense of rapport, of converse, though nothing had been said. He must have chosen friends in part at least on the basis of their capacity to pick up his psychic signals; those who did not would want to change him, and he would not change.

He had been writing before he came to Harvard. A sonnet "Thalia" had appeared in the Gardiner *Reporter Monthly*, and we know from letters that he was turning out a great deal of work, including translations from Virgil. The Harvard *Advocate* published two of his poems, "Ballade of the White Ship" and "Villanelle of Change," within two months of the opening of college. It looked like success. The poems themselves had very probably been written in Gardiner in the period of hard poetic exercise under the tutelage of Dr. Schumann. "In Harvard 5" came out shortly after these poems, and Robinson went around on invitation to meet the editors of the *Advocate,* surely for a period of about thirty years the most distinguished college literary magazine ever published. However high the young poet's hopes may have climbed, they would "come down presently." Coming back to his rooms, he told Saben he had been "unable to speak a word." The editors no doubt were like college editors today and always: quick, bright, glib and gregarious. If Robinson failed in their eyes, they failed equally in his: they could not pass his test of silence and were too busy making noise to pick up his signals. The incident is sad and instructive, because we can see in it both the source of much of Robinson's failure and the ground of his success as free spirit and poet.

The poems that Robinson must have been writing at this time we cannot certainly identify, and even those the *Advocate* published may well have had their beginnings in Gardiner. It seems likely however that most of the production of the Harvard years met destruction, and no doubt properly so. The poems mentioned above, all in the elaborate French forms Dr. Schumann had schooled his pupil in, bear the marks of apprenticeship and of the fin de siècle sort of poeticizing that Robinson was to parody, in the figure and the poetry of Killegrew in

Captain Craig. Although we can find, particularly in "Villanelle of Change" some evidence of the non or anti-poetic diction that came to be one Robinsonian innovation, little if any of the poetry which survives from the period and which we can identify as such has clear, unflawed merit. Possibly "The Night Before," one of the two poems whose titles make up that of Robinson's first book, had its genesis, as far as the actual writing goes, in the period shortly after he went to Cambridge. Chard Powers Smith in his "portrait" of the poet, as he calls his book, more than suggests that this poem comes directly from personal experience in the year 1880, that there was a first draft, now lost, that Robinson wrote a year or so later. The poem he finished in 1894 and which he never reprinted after its appearance in *The Torrent and the Night Before* (1896) at any rate belongs to the Harvard period if only because of its formal qualities of rhetoric, versification and general fin de siècle "passion."

Those Harvard years liberated Robinson, as a man and as a poet. In the college he found men who had seen something of the world and who did not subscribe to middle-class moral codes, in some sense aristocrats of the spirit who believed that freedom was not merely politics. The best evidence of the liberation can be found in Robinson's letters. There may be some posturing on occasion, but very little—far less than in most letters of great men. What we observe is the man's swift escape from moral clichés, particularly the sexual, and the opening of his mind and sensibility to what Harvard, Boston and Cambridge had to offer. The giants of the Harvard faculty in those days included, besides President Eliot himself, such figures as Francis Child, Josiah Royce, Lewis Gates, and above all William James. Charles Eliot Norton got the highest marks from Robinson, but he enjoyed Gates's lectures. Royce and he could never meet, since Robinson, like Henry James before him, confessed to a total incapacity for abstract reasoning all the more surprising in both artists since one is likely to impeach them almost above all others with abstracting to distraction. Robinson may have genuinely felt some of the impact of William James's thought, since it was in the air at Harvard and Harvard was then as later preeminently a place where thinking took precedence over all other efforts. And then, last of the philosophical triumvirate, there was George Santayana, the prodigy. He and Robinson do not ever seem to have met; they would have done one another good, though the likelihood of any meeting of minds is remote. By and large, it seems that though Harvard made a considerable mark on Robinson, he made none on Harvard nor on the influential students of his time. Only William Vaughn Moody, of those who would later achieve fame and do important work, could be in any sense called a friend, and the real friendship came later, in the years of Moody's success and Robinson's failure.

I would guess that Robinson wrote much and destroyed it all, or most of it, during those two years. The period had its discomforts for him, notably the sufferings he endured from mastoiditis, the consequences of a blow behind the ear given him as a schoolboy by a teacher. Moreover, he could not, however much he may have delighted in the theater and opera and concerts of Boston, in new friends, ideas and openings-up of experience, be oblivious to what was going on back home in the House on Lincoln Avenue. But at any rate, before the period of exile and tragedy very nearly finished him, he had those two years. They were not paradise, nor was Harvard the Oxford of Evelyn Waugh nor indeed the Harvard of T. S. Eliot, Conrad Aiken, Wallace Stevens. Which is in a way only to say two things: that ideas and poetry and the life of the mind and spirit fared badly in that age. Materialism, that mammon of unrighteousness, was never cursed more heartily by the prophets than by Robinson. It takes no seer to understand why. He suffered from it, directly, as directly as a man can: that is, he starved in the midst of plenty and he saw that the race went to the fixer, and much as he tried to summon humor, idealism and liquor to ease the pain, he could not get over it.

The other thing to say Henry James said at some length (and T. S. Eliot would echo him, along with others less notable). The old New England civilization had flowered and gone, leaving Brahminism, a kind of Arnoldian and raffinated "culture" which one saw in the best houses along with the Dresden, the Canton ware, the coin silver and the Sheraton chairs. They all came from ancestors and it was not to be considered that anything like another flowering (most disquieting thought) could ever take place. No, the cultivated of Boston, Cambridge and Harvard were custodians, janitors, as in a sense college professors are or should be. But Henry James remarks on the thinness of that New England culture, on its element of willed strenuousness which of course could only diminish and dwindle into eccentricity and looniness as the fine old blood ran thin. Boston and Cambridge were, as James felt them, rural in a way no country place could be—rural, and spiritually hick. The notorious Boston parochialism had and, vestigially, still has its charm; but for art to flourish, there must be, as Arnold observed, a coincidence of the man and the moment.

If Cambridge and Harvard were not for Robinson the place, nor 1891–93 the moment, neither was he the man for that time, those places. He himself said later that he came to Harvard expecting to "cut quite a shine as a poet . . . but Moody was in the field ahead of me. . . ." Moody would stay ahead—far ahead—until his untimely death, and both poets would stay rivals and conscious ones, though it is a tribute to both as men that they could honestly like and admire one another and one another's work. We have, if nothing else, Robinson's "The White Lights" to testify to his feeling for Moody's achievement in the success of *The Great Divide,* a play which he felt marked the beginning of a great period of drama in the country. But even this was still far ahead. Now, in 1892, in the spring, there was a warning note; the future would indeed have to take care of itself and Robinson with it—if that were allowed.

Edward Robinson died that spring. His youngest son went home to tend him at the last, and the old man died content, not knowing what was in store. What was in store worked itself out inexorably over the next few years, but meantime, with the House on Lincoln Avenue more like an O'Neill drama every month, Robinson could still get away for a second and final year at Harvard before the money, along with most things else, gave out. He worked reasonably hard that last year, published in the *Advocate* again, but only twice, one of the poems being a rather good sonnet, "Supremacy." When he left college for good in the spring of 1893, he seemed to know that he had left behind his youth and such of innocence as had been left him. Harvard would always remain for him the great good place.

What, finally, did he get from those two years? An impossible question which yet must be asked and, if not answered, certainly vexed a little. And for one thing, on the negative side, we can say simply that Cambridge wasn't Gardiner. It got him out of all that and it set him down among a body of men whose sophistication, experience and worldly circumstances must have startled, frightened, attracted and frustrated him by turns and all at once. That he should have been so tongue-tied with the literary set comes as no surprise to us; he was talkative only when half drunk, and that would come only in the desperate middle years. Shy, yes, of course; but with a genius for friendship, striking looking, clearly the gentleman with the fine, over-bred look of his overbred mother. Why could the *Advocate* set not see what must have been so obviously there? Perhaps it was not all that obvious to these young Brahmins and Proconsuls; if not, I for one suspect that they did not see it because Robinson was from up country, a nobody with no connections, no money and no prospects. Literature in Boston and at Harvard in those days was the province of aristocrats. An outsider took a long time to make the scene, and then only under impeccable auspices, as was so notably the case with William Dean Howells and Thomas Bailey Aldrich. I think Robinson, quite simply, was snubbed, both by the undergraduates and by certain donnish members of the faculty, just as I am inclined to think that the best element in Gardiner, with its close ties to the "great" of Boston, New York and England, would never make him more than a provisional and bohemian member of the set. Social snobbery administered by the adult world is bad enough; on the part of the young (and these young men were younger than he) it was and is intolerable. Among the young, the capacity for cruelty, all unconscious as it may be, is notorious. Robinson must have been its victim and as a result sought friends and solace with the outcast, as he would do for the rest of his life. Again and again critics and others have talked of Robinson's fascination with the theme of failure. I think the emphasis is misplaced. He learned very early, and college reinforced the lesson, that very very few people will love you for yourself alone. He saw, with that insight allowed only to the few, that there are those who are somebody, those who do something, those who are somebody *and* do something. He often felt himself to be nobody. As a poet, he must have felt that often enough. How does Keats describe the feeling?

It is a wretched thing to confess; but it is a very fact that not one word I ever utter can be taken for granted as an opinion growing out of my identical nature—how can it, when I have no nature? When I am in a room with People if I am ever free from speculating on creations of my own brain, then not myself goes home to myself: but the identity of everyone in the room begins to press upon me that I am in a very little time an(ni)hilated—not only among Men; it would be the same in a Nursery of children: I know not whether I make myself wholly understood: I hope enough so to let you see that no dependence is to be placed on what I said that day . . .

Robinson found himself between worlds, between literary eras, between societies, persons, places and things—the classic stance or, better, fate of the modern poet. He *knew* he was the best poet alive, but he was the only one who knew it, and who was he anyhow to know such a thing? Part of him was overbred, fine Big House New England, but on his father's side he was arriviste-bumpkin, the son of the "Duke of Puddledock." The air he breathed was promise-crammed and every pledge was broken. He loved failure as much as the rest of us do—and poverty! In the end, the best he could say was what he frequently said, that he could never have done anything but write poetry. I think he meant what Keats meant, that he never could be real to himself except as and when he was a poet. And what after all is a poet when he is not writing a poem? When he has finished a poem he is only, as Auden has put it, someone "who has finished a poem, perhaps for the last time." The work is all because of poetry and because the self exists only insofar as it makes poems. The point will come home to us forcefully when we consider Robinson's latter years and late work.

So he went back home to Gardiner, the House on Lincoln Avenue and the family. The money was going and would soon be gone; Edward Robinson had left financial affairs, even during his lifetime and retirement from business, to Herman, the wheeler-dealer who would, like Colonel Beriah Sellers, make everyone's fortune. Like Beriah Sellers, he had the desire and the plausibility but neither the ability nor the stamina. The depression of 1893 only compounded the errors Herman had made, and his patrimony and that of his brothers began to slip away from him, gradually at first, then more rapidly. And already Herman's solution to the problem was the time-honored one of drink. At first he had scurried west, tried to take charge, to liquidate some holdings and hang on to others till the tide should turn, but he simply did not have the resources, either of capital or nerve. In St. Louis in 1893 he was selling off holdings at auction; back in Gardiner he was as likely as not to drink a good bit of the day, spend much of the night out with "friends" and return home drunk. Emma Shepherd Robinson, Herman's wife, frequently stayed with her family in Farmingdale while Herman was on his travels; they had two daughters now and the time was coming when someone would have to take charge. For the moment, though, on Robinson's return from Cambridge, the time was ripe for poetry, and it seems that that summer, fall and winter, in the second floor back room of Lincoln Avenue, he divided his time between writing and either his "farming," which meant gardening and looking after the chickens, and such chores as cutting firewood and whatever else a house needs. Houses in that climate need a good deal.

It does not appear that he was unhappy. The poems began to come along. Now, for the first time, the Robinsonian portraitist-poet makes himself known, and equally, the transcendental poet, the oversold lover of universals starts his career. Throughout the years of his most fruitfully productive life both poets would seem to jog along, sometimes one leading, then the other, rarely pulling together and frequently running counter to one another's best achievement. From this period come Tilbury Town portraits, poems about other poets and writers, some of the direct personal statements such as the sonnet "Dear Friends." One resists pushing the autobiographical too far, yet the House on Lincoln Avenue, decaying New England and the decay of his own family before his very eyes—Dean, hopelessly addicted and very nearly a ghost, haunted the house in the flesh—must have had something to do with "The House on the Hill" and other "houses" in the long catalogue: Cavender's, Matthias', Old King Cole's, and above all that notable one with "the stairway to the sea," to mention only a few. The years between Harvard and New York, between 1893 and 1897, defined his art. If they saw the peculiar, original, and subtly penetrating Robinson style take shape, they equally provided the time for the poet to dwell on the quasi-mystical and to develop that Robinsonian version of Emersonitis best exemplified by the "Octaves" but notable in nearly all the later long narratives. Though we as readers may puzzle over why he found it necessary to puzzle his head with these things, one has finally to say that there can be only one answer: this groping after Truth, Unity, Weltanschauung or whatever which we might lump under the rubric Robinsonian Idealism, quite simply made up the ground of his being, the condition of his survival in a world of very nearly intolerable pain, frustration, hopelessness.

He had to watch his brother Dean go down, inevitably, and he had loved Dean deeply: "Dean knew more at twenty than I shall ever know," he said, and he meant it. As for Herman, the same inevitable decay was at work there, but Herman took more killing. Meanwhile there was the beautiful Emma, not to mention her small daughters. Then, only a few weeks before *The Torrent and the Night Before* arrived from the printers, Mary Robinson died. She had never really cared much about living after her husband's death, but her going was of a kind almost Jacobean in its horror. She had black diphtheria and no one— doctor, pastor, undertaker—would enter the house. Her sons ministered to her, the parson said a prayer through the window, the undertaker left a coffin on the porch and the three brothers buried their mother in the graveyard where Edward lay and where three years later Dean would go. Robinson said that he lived in hell, and few will quarrel with the statement.

How could anything have come out of such horror? If we can credit, as Chard Powers Smith in his *Where the Light Falls* demands that we do, the further dimension of New England Gothic that all three brothers were in love with Emma, that in particular Edwin loved her before, during and after Herman's pre-emption, then we have sheer melodrama. Mr. Smith makes the most of what he can find and he finds a lot, little of it convincing outside of a women's magazine but with enough of an air of plausibility to make Robinson's life seem not only a hell but one in which he so willingly immolated himself that it could only have been a pleasure. That it clearly lacked joy, Robinson's removal to New York would seem to prove. "There was nothing in the town below," the poet says with regard to Eben Flood. He knew it to be true of himself, so with six-hundred dollars from his father's estate, he left for "the town down the river," for the New York that from now on would be home, where in the long winters he would go into himself and dig out the poetry. He would come back to Gardiner for emergencies, visits, for a sight of his much loved nieces and their mother and of Mrs. Richards and her lively family. Indeed it was before he left that year that he met John Hays Gardiner (a Richards cousin) one of the Oaklands clan and a man who would be the poet's friend, admirer, and benefactor. Gardiner liked the poems and said so, the most direct way to a poet's heart; he had "no bigod nonsense about him" and made Robinson feel at ease, no mean feat. He taught literature at Harvard, but more than that, he liked it. A friend like that is perhaps as much as a poet can ask for, and this one had come unasked. It would be worthwhile coming back to Gardiner or Boston or Cambridge for him.

III

Steps to the Great Place

The Torrent and the Night Before cost fifty-two dollars to print at the Riverside Press in Cambridge. The little pamphlets came to Robinson and he sent them off to friends, critics, literary personages and magazines and waited for the results. They were negligible. The response to his work, in other volumes as well as this, would be an old, sad and ultimately squalid story if only because it seems to go on telling itself, poet after poet, time after time. It always in hindsight surprises us. Surely, we say, if one put a poem by George Edward Woodberry side by side with, say, "Luke Havergal," the meanest intellect would pick the latter. The meanest intellect might, but not the Literary Set dominating the taste of the magazines and quarterlies. Dear old Richard Watson Gilder, editor of the *Century,* was a dear man, but what did he care for such uncomfortable words? Boston critics and editors were like Boston women and their hats: they don't buy their hats; they *have* their hats. Only a few odd types of the sort Robinson seemed inadvertently to attract sensed that there was poetry in the book—and in subsequent books. Yvor Winters is unerring and deadly: "Nothing baffles the average critic so completely as honesty—he is prepared for everything but that; and I am under the impression that this has been true in every period." The honesty of Robinson's work is the point: nowhere does he fake it; even when he writes badly, he writes in ways that clearly belong to him and have a close resemblance to his best work. He writes sometimes mechanically, or self-indulgently, like any poet, particularly a Romantic poet;

and he wrote too much. "I've done far more than I ever dreamed of doing," he said just before his death. "When I got the first collected volume into my hands and turned the pages I was stupefied at the amount of it."

Readers today may feel a not wholly dissimilar stupefaction as they heft that grim, blocky tome that is the *Collected Poems* (1937). But in 1896, the rare creature who read Robinson read *The Torrent and the Night Before,* a small pamphlet with small type containing the poems which up to that time the poet cared to keep and which, with the important exception of "The Night Before," he would reprint, along with others, in the next book, *The Children of the Night* (1897). "Qui pourrai-je imiter pour être original?" A line from François Coppée and the epigraph to the book. Defiant, sardonic and to the modern perhaps baffling. Here was a young and unknown poet who did not even claim to be original—though the real joke was, of course, that he and he alone of all poets then writing in America had the best title to any such claim. And he knew it, if not then, surely later. And that a French writer, a prose writer too, should provide him with his epigraph has some significance, for it would seem that fiction has the most direct influence on at least one side of Robinson's work. If the writers we immediately think of here are Henry James and George Meredith we should not forget that Coppée, Maupassant and Daudet engrossed him in his formative years—at Harvard and in the years after in Gardiner. The prose, the fiction, that Robinson had always in view was shaped in large measure by the work of these men. If any poet can be said to have had a direct influence on this early published work, it might be Verlaine; beyond that, the Romantic style, with something of a Pre-Raphaelite cast, may be said to dominate rather than the idiom of a single poet.

What are these poems like? What are they for? How do some of them work? Questions requiring exploration, if not answers. Robinson dedicated this first book to "Any man, woman or critic who will cut the edges of it—I have done the top." Youthful bravado and all that, flip and not calculated to set well with the Richard Watson Gilders, the Thomas Bailey Aldriches and the three-name lady poets of the time. Still less would the poems themselves—if read at all. But that is another and a dreary story. Now is the time for us to read some of these very poems and to explore the questions they raise, beginning with "The Torrent."

> I found a torrent falling in a glen
> Where the sun's light shone silvered and leaf-split;
> The boom, the foam, and the mad flash of it
> All made a magic symphony; but when
> I thought upon the coming of hard men
> To cut those patriarchal trees away,
> And turn to gold the silver of that spray,
> I shuddered. Yet a gladness now and then
> Did wake me to myself till I was glad
> In earnest, and was welcoming the time
> For screaming saws to sound above the chime
> Of idle waters, and for me to know
> The jealous visionings that I had had
> Were steps to the great place where trees and torrents go.

First of all, it puts the central concern of Robinson's personal and poetic lives directly to us: "Where trees and torrents go." Where do they go and where come from? All his life long he would, in the manner of his New England forebears, familial and poetic, vex himself and that question, occasionally to good purpose, more often perhaps to none or at least to such as we can no longer respond to. The poem is seminal; it is closely observed; it thinks well on the page until the last leap in the last line when we must, like the speaker of the poem, either accept or go down. Ordinarily one does not think of Robinson as a poet who notices, admires and reproduces in words natural objects and scenes, yet as a matter of fact such scenes do exist and vitally in many of the better poems, as a circumambience or a cyclorama for the play, an environment out of which characters emerge and to which they return. "The Torrent" deals with environment as symbol. Coming out of a wilderness, it falls in "foam" with "boom" and "flash" to make a symphonic effect, beautiful but soon to die or to be put to the uses of factory and mill. The image of fall will recur in Robinson's work many times; here, the fall is out of innocence into the world of "hard men," and yet, the transcendental now asserting itself, this too will give way, prove to be "steps to the great place where trees and torrents go."

What place is that? He does not tell us and he does not know but he knows that we must either believe it is there and work toward it in belief, or "seizing the swift logic of a woman / Curse God and die," as he has it in "The Man Against the Sky." What will compel our acceptance of the leap concluding this poem will be, I think, persuasion by the facts of the case: the waterfall, the glen, the leaves, the "scream" of the power saws which will turn those "idle" waters to polluted and profitable courses. Like it or not, the poem seems to say (and the poet does not like it) all this beauty will give way to the exigencies of economics because the time and the age will have it so. Yet they themselves will pass, will prove steps to the great place. And what place is that? We must ask Luke Havergal himself.

That poem seems to have puzzled Robinson as being one of his first that might be almost called "popular," and like many another poet before and since, the popularity annoyed him because he would have liked the accolade to go to poems in which he felt himself more fully involved. "Luke Havergal" is one of those lucky hits, on the whole uncharacteristic of its author, which any poet may pray for but which strike at random and seem to the author insultingly gratuitous as the result of a cause incommensurate with the considerable effect. "Here I have been slaving for weeks or months on this piece of most calculated, most severely exercised craftsmanship—and *you* come along with your damned foreign airs and get away with the whole thing in an hour. Unfair." Reviewers at the time and later tended to single out this poem as remarkable. Indeed it is. Robinson himself spoke of it patronizingly as an "uncomfortable abstraction" and an apparently contrived exercise in "degeneration." For all that, the poem has roots in the Decadence of the 'nineties, in the symbolic mode, and in that ground of Robinson's conviction in which grew such grim and potent plants as "For A Dead Lady," "Eros Turannos," "Lost Anchors," to name but three. For "Luke Havergal" shows us that "the great place" may in fact be hell. The leaves that flashed in sunlight have turned to "crimson on the wall," and the "western gate" where Luke must pass need not lead to paradise. Let him choose and go: he will find out where he has gone when he gets there. In any case, it can be no worse than where he is. If, as Chard Powers Smith says, the poem dates absolutely from the Harvard years, then it is a very young man's poem, decadent if not "degenerate," yet wholly objectified, firm, closer to Baudelaire than to the Verlaine who may possibly have influenced it.

Leaves, fall, and falling. Here again that season of the year, that time of day, that downward movement, dying fall. The upward thrust and the descent again and again set the bounds of a poem's movement and of Robinson's own cosmology, if I may use that term out of unwillingness to say "philosophy." "The Master," "For a Dead Lady," "Eros Turannos," "Mr. Flood's Party" and countless others all show ascent or decline or both, specifically or by implication or both, in dramatic encounter or image or both. But in this first volume, the themes he would explore at large or in brief shape themselves clearly and finally. The Robinson of, let us say, such a late narrative poem as *Amaranth* gives images of decay and desolation as he did nearly forty years before in "The House on the Hill," and in both cases the houses are Maine houses, Gardiner Big Houses. The hope clung to in "The Torrent" is asserted once again, and for the last time, in *King Jasper* (1935); moreover, here we first see the range of subject matter; if not fully in this first small book, then certainly in the next, which is but a reissue of the first with "The Night Before" omitted and sixteen new poems added. That book, called *The Children of the Night,* adds, significantly, the "Octaves"; hence we can say that we have therein examples of everything Robinson would attempt in verse except the blank verse narrative. "Octaves" he would never attempt again, and in this volume they may fairly be said to represent something of the blank verse speculation that would engage him so completely in the latter years, as well as combining in themselves elements of the sonnet and the lyric. They make as it were a bridge between his speculative sonnets, of which there are a number in this book, and the blank verse narrative. Without characters, actions or situation, unrhymed and yet with lines so endstopped that they seem to cry out for rhyme, the "Octaves" represent one of Robinson's curious lapses, I think; his eye and ear have failed him and he pursues here not a subject and a poetic idea but an abstraction, a transcendental, a matter which we shall investigate more fully later on.

On the other hand, there are the Tilbury Town folk, a various crew, some of them memorable like John Evereldown, some of them survivors only of what EA himself called "anthological pickle" like Richard Cory, and a few more than that, like Reuben Bright and the clerks in the sonnet of that title, not forgetting of course Luke Havergal. These dramatis personae would have made the reputation of another poet; had Robinson given them foreign names and put them somewhere in Provence or the Mediterranean basin, what a difference it might have made. But he "told it like it was," and he had never been to Europe, could not fake it enough to deceive himself into an attempt. His Muse had indeed migrated from Greece and Ionia, and in doing so became herself again with a new classicism that came not out of books alone but out of nature and civilization.

Some years later Robinson would publish a volume of his *Sonnets* (1928), and though we would have to say they are a mixed bag, we would also have to acknowledge that he does things with the form that had not been done. The best of them, like the best of the poems in *The Children of the Night*, have roots in character, time and place. A number deal with writers: Crabbe, Zola, Verlaine, Thomas Hood, of which the first and the last seem to me not only the best but among his finest achievements in the form. A sonnet tends to make trouble, as best exemplified by the remark made to Laura E. Richards by Kate Vannah, one of the ladies of Gardiner who was in the literary set that had taken in EA: "He says it takes him six weeks to write a sonnet. It takes me ten minutes. One of us is crazy." One feels sure Robinson would have been the first to admit to the craziness; what else is a poet for? Nor would he ever have contended that work in and of itself makes a poem; we have the sonnet-writing competition between Leigh Hunt and Keats to prove that what counts in the short run as well as the long is genius—which is, I take it, at least in part a tendency to have good luck in a particular course of endeavor. The best of Robinson's sonnets take an anti-rhetorical line though they often ride to eloquence as they progress. Frequently, though, as for example in "Reuben Bright," the eloquence comes from keeping a steady eye on character firmly and economically established, then put under pressure, and at last disposed of. Reuben Bright is "placed" in the first line and given authenticity and dimension in the second; lines three and four involve him with us as readers, lines five through eight immerse him in the plot, and we want to know what happens next.

> Because he was a butcher and thereby
> Did earn an honest living (and did right)
> I would not have you think that Reuben Bright
> Was any more a brute than you or I;
> For when they told him that his wife must die,
> He stared at them, and shook with grief and fright,
> And cried like a great baby half that night,
> And made the women cry to see him cry.

Now, so far, not so good I hear a critic crying: a sonnet is not an O. Henry story, and haven't we heard "Richard Cory" before? The rejoinder goes: Read the poem and forget about Greece and Ionia and Provence—very good places indeed but not on the itinerary. And besides, have you read any Hopkins lately? A sonnet is to a poet of power what a word was to Humpty Dumpty: "It is a question of who is to be master." The sonnet was made for poets, not poets for the sonnet. In this specific case of the sonnets in *The Children of the Night,* we find at least three of his best, which is really to say three of the best by any American poet. These are "The Clerks," "Reuben Bright" and "The Pity of the Leaves." The last is a remarkable poem if only for the originality of the theme and the subject. Here we see one of the few cases of direct influence of Robinson on Frost and on a school of New England epigoni. The subject is an old man in an old house; the theme, loss, loneliness and a sense of guilt and remorse. The provenience has Hawthorne in it, no doubt; the visual imagery comes from a scene almost as common now as in Robinson's own time: an old man alone in a decaying house somewhere in the Maine countryside. Frost and perhaps R. P. T. Coffin explored this theme much more obviously, and Frost would give the general theme original and remarkable twists in "The Witch of Coös" and other shorter poems. Coffin in his *New Poetry of New England* points out various correspondences between each poet's treatment of theme and subject. What makes "The Pity of the Leaves" more than usually powerful derives from Robinson's sense of the old man's implication in an "ancestral shame." If we take the better stories of Sarah Orne Jewett as the locus classicus for the genre here adverted to—the old man or woman alone in an old house in New England—we have the origin of the idea in its specifically Maine form. Again, Hawthorne must be acknowledged the true innovator, but by late in the nineteenth century a specifically rural Maine version was to arise, degenerating into some of the less credible quasi-Freudian projections of O'Neill. Worse would come!

The Pity of the Leaves

Ven_ ful across the cold November moors
Loud with ancestral shame there came the bleak
Sad wind that shrieked, and answered with a shriek
Reverberant through lonely corridors.
The old man heard it; and he heard, perforce,
Words out of lips that were no more to speak—
Words of the past that shook the old man's cheek
Like dead remembered footsteps on old floors.

And then there were the leaves that plagued him so!
The brown, thin leaves that on the stones outside
Skipped with a freezing whisper. Now and then
They stopped and stayed there—just to let him know
How dead they were, but if the old man cried,
They fluttered off like withered souls of men.

Miss Jewett once said that when an old woman and an old house came together in her head "with a click," she knew she had a story. "The Only Rose," one of the most remarkable of many stories in the genre, admirably illustrates her statement. Always she risks the worst kind of sentimentality because of what I. A. Richards once called "mnemonic irrelevancies": we bring to theme and subject our own memories, real or imagined, of such events, which in turn prompt the author to deal largely in clichés and sentiment, "tears and flapdoodle" as Huck Finn

put it. Miss Jewett fails at times and the pity and terror turn
to bathos. It may be that Robinson wrote some bad poetry,
but sentimental verse was beyond him; when a poem on this
particular theme and subject does fail, it fails from a kind of
tricky forcing of the "plot"; it turns melodramatic or simply a
bit slick, as in "The Whip" or perhaps "Richard Cory," though
that poem would need less defense if it could be retired from
all anthologies for a few seasons. But here, in "The Pity of the
Leaves," Robinson writes in one of his best veins. In Miss
Jewett, we find only the ingredients of frustrated feeling, loneliness and the regenerative power of love, or the lack of it. Here,
the "ancestral shame," never actually specified, clings to the poem,
takes reinforcement from the implication of personal guilt:
"words of the past." These apply equally to ancestors and to
the old man himself and his dead family; they remind us, these
words and the "leaves" with which they become associated, of
the words and leaves in "Luke Havergal." But the two poems
are very little alike: the latter has a movement, and a symbolic
structure, rather more "decadent," grotesque and lurid than the
former, which alternates the old man's own ruminative, querulous
tone with the "shriek" of the wind and the "freezing whisper"
of the leaves.

I might say that I pick these three sonnets for the reason that
I tend to admire most of Robinson's poems that deal with
person, place and thing—they have an anchor in the senses,
do not speculate on vast imponderables, and leave to the concrete imaginings of the reader such of implication and symbolic resonance as he can contrive after some acquaintance with
the poetry. "Reuben Bright" may or may not have been an
actual butcher and citizen of Gardiner, but we can see and feel
him cry "like a great baby half that night." As so often happens,
tone establishes the general range of our attitudes and feelings,
and the tone is both detached and ambiguously ironic. That
simple parenthesis at the end of line two—"(and did right)"—
gives us pause, particularly if we know anything at all about
Robinson's own feelings about earning a living; in the context
of his life, of the time, of the American scene, the phrase has
more weight than might appear. Similarly, in the sestet Reuben
has paid off "the singers and the sexton *and the rest*" (my italics)

before he puts away his wife's things and tears down the slaughterhouse.

> And after she was dead and he had paid
> The singers and the sexton and the rest,
> He packed a lot of things that she had made
> Most mournfully away in an old chest
> Of hers, and put some chopped-up cedar boughs
> In with them, and tore down the slaughter-house.

What does the reader make of "the rest"? Who are they? The phrase is intended to stand for more than undertakers and supernumeraries of whatever exsequious sort; he pays other debts as well. The very calculated vagueness here sets the imagination going, but lest we go too far out, Robinson brings us back with that final, brutal, low-keyed declaration, "and tore down the slaughter-house." Oddly, a misprint at once laughable and infuriating cropped up in the first printing: "down *to* the slaughter house!" One can still find it here and there, and a few critics have singled it out for Irony and Pity. That aside, the conclusion of this sonnet, while superficially vulnerable perhaps to accusations of melodrama and affectation, works well because it has been prepared and because the tone of the poem carries the "plot" dispassionately along. The poet never predisposes us beforehand either against or for the protagonist, yet the very achieved distance—distancing, in effect—reinforces the ironies we have observed. Reuben Bright becomes Everyman, absorbed in the ordinary brutal round of getting on, who yet has powerful if inarticulate feeling.

The view taken here strikes me as remarkable in so young a man as Robinson was when he wrote it: the sympathy and the insight into ordinariness one rarely associates with intelligent youth. But I suppose Robinson, like most fine poets, came at such sympathy by way of his métier: the very art of poetry taught him about life, rather than the other way around. The third sonnet I have mentioned seems to me to clinch the point, though the reader of these pages and of "The Clerks" might fault me for riding the hobby-horse too hard and far. At any rate, it seems to me that the clerks must surely be old friends of Robinson's from Gardiner days (Note, by the way, how Robinson, like Eliot, so often makes himself seem old and disenchanted) who have never fulfilled the promise of their youth—or better, have fulfilled it entirely by growing old. He could see, even in his twenties, some of his friends slipping into the pattern of small-town commerce. We can take the term "clerk" as a generic one for any man involved in commercial enterprise below what the contemporary jargon styles "the executive level," though I am by no means sure Robinson rules out such exalted types. Be that as it may, these clerks are men, both good and human—as good and as human "as they ever were." If Robinson had ended his poem with the octave, we might have doubts as to his sympathy; irony leaks out from the description of the men with their "shop-worn brotherhood," a phrase which evokes Kiwanis and Rotary, while the final phrase of the octave "as they ever were" cuts two ways: how good were they, ever?

The sestet answers: as good as you and I, then, now or later! The speaker of the poem clearly involves himself in the human disaster of living: "poets and kings," you and I, all of us high, low and in between, are "clerks of Time." That very capacity to understand without sentimentality, to maintain a moral view without rigidity, to face reality without showing off about it: these attitudes and capacities demand the ironic tone, and irony can be both misunderstood and misapplied when it deals with common life and affairs. Many of Robinson's poems were thus misunderstood for a very long time. *The Children of the Night* disappeared in the wastes of pop poetry with no trace. Five years were to pass before another book would appear, subsidized by friends—as the first two were what we call today "vanity publications." In those intervening years, Robinson would leave Gardiner to all intents forever, the family would disintegrate finally, and he would very nearly starve to death. It would be more years still before any publisher would willingly touch his work and before he would have an existence more than barely marginal.

IV

The Town Down the River

His first invasion of New York lasted only six weeks and could not be called a success. For all his experience in obscurity, he could not, with youth, ambition and his genius, help hoping that someone would respond, doors would open, he would, like the protagonist of "Old Trails," "saunter into fame." He joined his college friend Burnham in a rooming house on West 64th Street and set about trying to make literary connections which would be of service to him and his poetry. Such few lines as were open to him promised very little, really. There was the egregious Titus Munson Coan, who had written to Robinson in praise of *The Torrent and the Night Before,* and since the poet had answered the letter there was an acquaintance of sorts to presume upon. Coan had collected about him a set of intellectual and artistic drifters and hangers-on, among them William Henry Thorne and Craven Langstroth Betts, a Nova Scotian who had been lightly touched by a muse and would never recover. He became a good friend of Robinson's by the initial and simple measure of telling him that he liked his poetry a great deal. But perhaps above all there was Alfred H. Louis, a most extraordinary figure who would put a permanent mark on Robinson by virtue of his shadowy past, his fallen present, his indomitable spirit. He became the original of Captain Craig and he appears, as it were glancingly, in other poems, most notably "The Wandering Jew." He seems to have been one of those men who really had done many important things, had got to the very edge of true fame, and then, for inscrutable reasons

(reasons only Freudians would care to investigate) turned away, headed down and kept on going. He dominated, by the power of talk and intellect and learning, the circle about Coan; the aura of Cambridge, and of lofty connections with Gladstone and George Eliot and the *Spectator* clung about him. He truly dazzled his hearers, as Algernon Blackwood shows in *Episodes Before Thirty*. The meeting of this legendary, nearly incredible creature and the poet would have its effect, but not yet. Robinson had to go home to tend his dying brother Dean, so back he went to Gardiner and the House on Lincoln Avenue. It would be long before he could exorcise all those ghosts.

The House on Lincoln Avenue was not welcoming. In the first place, the spectacle of Dean might daunt anyone, but particularly a brother who had idolized this boyhood hero. And then there was Herman who, according to Chard Powers Smith's account, was jealous of the affection or whatever it was that his wife Emma and the poet felt for one another. If he did not forbid him the house, so to speak, he made matters uncomfortable enough so that Robinson seems to have shifted about between the nearby town of Winthrop and Cambridge, and visits to friends. In the summer of 1898 he was back in Gardiner, where he seems to have had some kind of affair with a female whom Smith coyly and unhelpfully calls the Woodland Girl. This particular nymph seems to have been a friend or relation of the Oakland Gardiners who for all her charm, aristocratic Brahminism and hard cash, either did not care to marry a penniless poet of dubious antecedents, or else let her elegant family do the obvious. But it may equally well be the case that Robinson no more wanted to marry her than he appears to have wanted marriage with any woman. Both Hagedorn and Smith touch on this matter, Smith in considerable detail, but most readers would, I believe, feel that considering the matter all round, family pressure and the poet's own self-doubt would be quite enough to account for the breaking-off of the affair, if affair it was.

Mostly, Robinson during this year read, saw his friends and accumulated the material for poems. One would give a good deal to know more of his inner life, at this time and at others. It seems to have been a seminal year—a bridge between the past work, much of it promising and some truly achieved, and what would come later. He should perhaps have stayed in Cambridge and Boston, where he might well have found the men and women who could and would help him in his career and see to it that he made a bare living. I can only guess at what went on in his head during this time, but perhaps he wanted New York, because there he felt wholly anonymous. All the past could recede and never touch him, while it remained available for poetry. Boston, Cambridge and Gardiner had reality and held friends, enemies, and memories too near for use. He must get away, and away meant New York. He later said that New York meant, as it were, gestation; he went there to let the poetry grow and develop. Boston and particularly the MacDowell Colony in Peterborough, New Hampshire, were the places where poetry got written. He wrote slowly and the poems took a long time to grow. Unlike such poets as Eliot and Stevens, Robinson could never do anything but write poetry, as he said so often, and the combination of banking or insurance with poetry would never have been possible for him, even had an opportunity presented itself. John Hays Gardiner got him a job as a kind of assistant to President Eliot of Harvard, and though he enjoyed living in Cambridge again, he hated being a kind of superior janitor and did not like President Eliot, who apparently told him he should get married—*pour encourager les autres,* presumably. Theodore Roosevelt gave him a job in the New York Customs to save him from starvation. Robinson not only showed no gratitude but ignored Roosevelt's first overtures to the point of provoking the great man to ask him pathetically what he might be allowed to do to help. When Robinson took the job, he did not bite the hand that fed him. He did worse. He ignored it and wrote no poetry.

His inner life must have been intense, as is that of all literary artists. Yet here we need to show caution. It would be, I think, a mistake to assume that a poet's inner life concerns itself with vast ideas, great truths, profundities of all descriptions. Again, Keats and his description of the poet and the poetic faculties come to mind. It is the *anonymity,* the seemingly calculated erasure of character and personality which mark the poetic nature, by this account of it. Robinson had always kept quiet and his own counsel. True, he would talk late into the night with a few friends and after a few drinks; he always felt more comfortable in a small group than a large, and he had really no social life in the accepted sense of that expression. Even when he was at Harvard small talk made him uneasy—he had no capacity for it himself and could not conceive how others could not only engage in idle chitchat but apparently enjoy it. A matter of temperament, at least in part. But his experience and upbringing would naturally accentuate a condition common enough among poets and perhaps best shown in Thomas Mann's "Tonio Kröger." By self-discipline and as a result of success many poets have learned to be, or appear to be, at home in salons, the White House, and generally among the pillars of the Establishment. They can be just as prudential as the next man—rather more so in many cases. Because they have succeeded in some small way in attracting attention, if only as a kind of court jester, they can overcome some part of the innate reserve, shyness, insecurity—what you will—that goes with the poetic territory. Robinson had no chance to become one of these. He had few ties with society, in the larger and smaller senses of the word. He had no stake in it. He lived most of his mature life as an outcast on the fringes of New York bohemia, without wife, child, or relation of any kind, except his nieces and their mother back in Gardiner, a town he no doubt wished he could forget had it not been for them and Mrs. Richards. When success came, it came too late, for the man and for the poetry, and though he enjoyed being taken up by the rich and powerful, he could no longer have made use of them. They could give him nothing any more.

Yet that is not the whole story. Robinson's inner life, like anyone else's, will and must remain a mystery, but we do know enough about his time—we know enough of person, place and thing—to sense that here we have a case of exacerbated New Englandism of the kind Emily Dickinson exemplifies. Allen Tate has put it finely and completely, I think, in his essay. As he sums it up, the New England idea "dramatized the human soul." Only in New England has life been seen as a struggle, not between man and nature or between man and man, but between man and the dark powers, in himself and all about him. Tate shows effectively how the great theocratic experiment in New England broke up under the impact of commerce and industry and how no longer could Calvinist strenuousness and rigidity of doctrine inform, contain and keep coherent a people and the individual character:

> The Gilded Age had already begun. But culture in the true sense, was disappearing. Where the old order, formidable as it was, had held all this personal experience, this eclectic excitement, in a comprehensible whole, the new order tended to flatten it out in a common experience that was not quite in common; it exalted more the personal and the unique in the interior sense. Where the old-fashioned puritans got together on a rigid doctrine, and could thus be individualists in manners, the nineteenth-century New Englander, lacking a genuine religious center, began to be a social conformist. The common idea of the Redemption, for example, was replaced by the conformist idea of respectability among neighbors whose spiritual disorder, not very evident at the surface, was becoming acute. A great idea was breaking up, and society was moving towards external uniformity, which is usually the measure of the spiritual sterility inside.

Here again, caution: Emily Dickinson and Edwin Arlington Robinson do not necessarily stand for, or in some way exemplify, the spiritual plight of fin de siècle New England nor the crisis of the Protestant conscience. Yet they share an unease and a quality of the exacerbated spirit that belong not only to the time, place and culture but which seem peculiarly American. We have seen something of it in Hawthorne; Allen Tate says of Emily Dickinson that "her life was one of the richest and deepest ever lived on this continent." The paradox strikes one instantly. How can a foiled, frustrated and apparently maimed spirit live anything like such a life? The time in which a poet lives has much to do with the sorts of lives available for him to lead, but even more than that, it contains the store of ideas or images which he is able to comprehend, for a poet is not a creator but a maker, and he works with what there is. Again, Allen Tate has something to say about Emily Dickinson's situation which has exemplary value:

A culture. . . . is an available source of ideas that are imbedded
in a complete and homogeneous society. The poet finds himself
balanced upon the moment when such a world is about to fall,
when it threatens to run out into looser and less self-sufficient
impulses. This world order is assimilated, in Miss Dickinson, as
mediaevalism was in Shakespeare, to the poetic vision; it is
brought down from abstraction to personal sensibility.

"When such a world is about to fall." Enough time elapsed
between Emily Dickinson's and Robinson's productive years
for that world to have fallen entirely into decay. The collapse
was total, and in the history of Robinson's personal life, as
well as in that of his surroundings, lies a good deal of material
for poetry. That he used much of it seems plain. The Gardiner
of Robinson's childhood and youth, his family and its fate,
the falling from decay to disaster that was the story of Maine
towns had of necessity, one must suppose, an impact on the
poet's sense. The decayed Big House, the "house on the hill,"
the rotting wharves all find their poetic rendering in the verse,
and of course the human wreckage abounds. In the Arthurian
trilogy Robinson writes of collapse, the collapse of an empire,
the "wrecked empire" of *Merlin,* the smash of the old order
World War I brought about.

If that were all, if Robinson's poetry merely reflected the time,
he would be no more remarkable a poet than many another,
Moody for one, but there is much more, and perhaps we sense
it best in the tension, so omnipresent with Robinson, between
the abstract and the immediately specific. Tate observes of
Emily Dickinson that she had, strictly speaking, no ideas and
no opinions. "O for a life of sensations rather than thoughts,"
says Keats. Emily Dickinson felt thoughts as they came to her
in the forms of her inherited Calvinist culture. Ideas came to
her as sensation. She had no capacity whatever for abstract
thought. Tate points out that Hawthorne did have such a
capacity and it undoes him frequently. Henry James, discussing
in *Notes of a Son and Brother* his brief career at Harvard Law
School, speaks of his own total incapacity to think abstractly.
Robinson belongs with all these writers, but perhaps more with
Hawthorne than the other two, if only because he saw more of
the world of men and suffering and could not "live in art" in

the ways both Emily Dickinson and James could. Like Hawthorne, he moved between worlds, and like Hawthorne, too,
he vexed heaven with his quest for transcendental value. Unlike
Hawthorne, he could never learn to get on without it, to find
comfort in a stripped-down, naked vision of reality. Perhaps
the comfortless life he led forced him from a sense of self-
preservation to assert his "idealism" in the face of what might
otherwise seem overwhelming evidence of brute materiality.
Religion had for both men ceased to exist. As Hawthorne could
scarcely tolerate the ecstasies of Jones Very and the fauna of
Brook Farm, so Robinson has only the barest sympathy for the
self-deluding inhabitants of "the wrong world" of *Amaranth*.
No doubt early religious training in a truly religious time and
place might have solaced him, but the Gardiner of his young
years had the standard proper Congregationalism for the rank
and file, Anglican Episcopalianism for the nobs and nabobs,
and "damn-all" for everyone else, except the Canucks who had
their barbarous Roman Catholicism. The poet's own forebears
on his mother's side had all been Congregationalists, and the
Scotch-Irish Robinsons had been Presbyterian once. The young
Robinson lived in a family of occasional churchgoers; Mary
Robinson went to church, but it does not appear that her son
remembered much more about going there himself as a boy
than that he liked the singing when there was any. But then,
he liked almost any singing. Of course, all through life he read
the Bible, though not as his forebears and even his mother might
have wished. He wrote to Mrs. Richards that "Jehovah is
positively the worst character in fiction," an ambiguously ironic
remark that among other things tells us how seriously he took
the matter of man's relations with his maker, if any. He surely
would have endorsed the statement of the old Garibaldino in
Conrad's *Nostromo* that religion is for women and God for men.
In his later years, at any rate. In his earlier days Emersonianism
played hell with his life and his poetry and would in fact in-
trude throughout his career. The New England Appetite for
Universals, conveniently stripped of any particular applicability,
seemed not only a compulsion but a kind of savior.

It will not do to make fun of the tendency. If overindulgence
in it gave us the "Octaves" and some of the arid narratives,

that same desire for "the light" that is everywhere in *Lancelot* emerged in many of the better lyrics. Light imagery of various sorts marks out many of the poems, "Luke Havergal" for one leading instance.

> No, there is not a dawn in eastern skies
> To rift the fiery night that's in your eyes;
> But there, where western glooms are gathering,
> The dark will end the dark, if anything.

Like most folk of powerfully religious forebears—and with no saving mixture with other racial types—Robinson possessed, or was possessed by, what G. B. Shaw called the "metaphysical appetite." The story of New England's theocracy so beautifully told by Hawthorne is still to tell; some of Robinson's long poems continue the tale. In his own life he tried to exorcise the ghost of orthodox Calvinism and pretty well succeeded; he eventually went to the psychiatrist-poet Merrill Moore for help, but that was late in life. He tried table-tipping, Christian Science, Freud—what today the jargon calls "the whole bit," simply because his appetite drove him and he could not rest in the mindless, behavioristic materialism that to him represented as it were the anti-Christ. We may today find difficulty understanding what he meant when, after a session of "table-tipping" with his father during the latter's last illness, the table did indeed tip, "cutting my universe clean in half." Whether or not that particular event did the cutting, his universe took on the New England duality: flesh this side, spirit that. Emerson may be the most obviously guilty party, but William Ellery Channing and a host of metaphysical speculators share the blame. What Emerson could not abide about Jones Very was that he saw angels: he didn't "imagine" them or fancy them; like Blake, he *saw* them. They were real—more real than Emerson and Bronson Alcott.

The split between man and god, flesh and spirit, becomes readily enough a split between art and life, the merely useful and the merely good, beautiful and true. That, rather than the theme of failure, obsessed Robinson and gave rise to the vague "spirituality" of certain characters in the long poems, *Lancelot* for one. Since Robinson had no religion, only an appetite for the transcendent, he had no belief, only convictions; no symbols for his metaphysical speculations, only vague images such as "light." When, however, he deals with a particular person under particular spiritual stress, the symbols start up from the very ground of the person's being and from the physical counterpart of the stress. One of the most striking instances occurs in the last line of "The Gift of God," where the "roses thrown on marble stairs" take on pathos, irony, and a bitter wit. The juxtaposition of the stairs and roses gives both a dramatic and a symbolic intensity, in that the one sardonically refers to the insubstantiality of dream, and the other to the exuberance of a maternal love. What, in fact, one tends to realize after a long reading of Robinson's poetry is that the blood had run thin: racial, religious, traditional, rhetorical. The whole supply had been used up by the great ancestors. It remained for the last of the line to close the door on the ancestral house because "there is nothing more to say." When Robinson writes out of a deep conviction of loss, loneliness, stoic pride, and sometimes out of sheer memory, he writes superlatively—because he thinks as a poet should and knows what poets know. Only when he confronts ancestral and youthful memories or archetypes of experience which he could feel deeply does he make a new language out of the old and see a world "radiant with his own delight." The delight will be qualified with irony, with the sense Eben Flood has that "most things break," but miraculously that makes delight and all such things dearer.

V

Down and Out

The meeting with Alfred Louis was fatal to Robinson, though to Louis it gave immortality of a kind. The old man whom he met at Coan's curious establishment haunted him, and out of that meeting and the subsequent friendship, not to mention the repercussions thereof, came the ill-starred *Captain Craig*. Louis fascinated Robinson by his "untempered eloquence," his legendary past, and his truly absurdist mingling of best philosopher and charlatan. There was no telling fact from fiction in his saga, nor did Robinson try; he found a subject for a long poem, his first. What happened to it has saga qualities in its own right.

Robinson knew by this time, in Cambridge in 1899, that he had hold of something, that whatever happened he had the gift and the staying power. He could not foresee wholly how terrible would be that knowledge. He had begun *Captain Craig* and would in a sense stake his reputation on the volume of that title and on that particular poem in particular as the set piece, the obligatory performance, the major work by the young poet. No more "promise" as reviewers say, but fulfillment, pressed down and running over. He could not foresee that three years would pass before a group of his friends, with Mrs. Richards at their head, would succeed in bludgeoning a publisher, in this case Houghton Mifflin, into accepting the manuscript and then only when costs had been guaranteed. Nor could the poet know that for several months while he was trying to get Small Maynard to accept or reject or even return his poems, that poor waif was in a Boston whorehouse in the custody of the madam, a sympathetic soul who cared more for poetry than the editor who had forgotten his package. Perhaps he found the whorehouse so like a publishing house that he got confused. When he returned there he got the manuscript back, and Robinson got it back too. The story is grotesque. Had it happened to Baudelaire, we would find an appropriately raffish rivegaucherie about the episode, but it happened in Boston and to Edwin Arlington Robinson, a fact which seems harder to deal with.

Captain Craig had several aims, it appears. When it finally appeared in 1902 and fell into a void, something really died in Robinson, I think. He went down. Not all the way nor finally, but down as far as one can go into penury and drink without starvation on the one hand and alcoholism on the other. He would say later on that it was the fact that he did not exist as a poet that seemed so hard to bear, that it did not matter so much that critics and others were hostile as that they ignored him: he did not exist. When after several years he finally came back to the light, he had been a long way and the experience marked him.

Theodore Roosevelt got him a job in the New York Customs. The story of how that came about has some significance, inasmuch as it not only demonstrates the fortuitousness of patronage but also marks the last attempt at such by a President. Roosevelt's son Kermit, a student at Groton School, had as a teacher of English Henry Richards, the son of Laura E. Richards and an admirer of Robinson's poetry. Young Kermit picked up a copy of *Captain Craig* from his teacher's· desk and became fascinated. In due course he told his father, who in his turn read the book and took pains to find out something about Robinson and his way of life. The aristocratic connections the Richards family enjoyed did Robinson some service; one doubts that Roosevelt would have bestirred himself in behalf of a poet less impeccably recommended. At any rate, having found out how it was with Robinson and his condition, the President approached the poet directly, with a view to "locating" him advantageously. The poet declined the gambit. After one or two other abortive attempts at uplift, Roosevelt finally wrote and asked him directly, and rather piteously, what he might do to help him. The net result was a five-year stint for Robinson in the New

York Customs House, where he presumably did even less work than even Hawthorne in his comparable post. But from 1905 until the change in administration and consequent change of policy and personnel in 1909, Robinson spent more or less time, usually less, daily at his office, where he read the paper, always leaving it behind to show that he had been there. Poets and other writers would have to wait until another Roosevelt to find federal employment.

The Customs job came in the nick of time for Robinson. Before that he had lived on handouts from friends, worked as a timekeeper in the subway then under construction, drank himself into either good spirits or sleep every night. The only thing that saved him, he said himself, was that he never took a drink before six. Roosevelt got Scribners to reissue *The Children of the Night* in 1905. It would be 1910 before *The Town Down the River*, the first book he would publish without subsidy and outside pressure: for the first time a book that was not a "vanity press job"!

Why? We all know that poets are supposed to have a hard time, but this is ridiculous! Nowadays, when anyone seems to be able to publish anything (not that anyone reads it), we have trouble understanding how and why it happened as it did. I think the reasons are fairly obvious, and the most apparent is that the poet and his work came into being in Matthew Arnold's period of between worlds—one dead, the other powerless to be born. Literary people quite simply could not understand what Robinson was about because they sensed that what he was saying was somehow uncomfortable, that it wanted them to look at objects, attitudes, people and events which had not been considered poetic, and withal in a language too like what they thought of as prose for them to feel that it could be "beautiful." The reviewers who took him to task for being a "pessimist" and for seeing the world as a "prison-house" really meant that Robinson told the truth and they did not want to hear it, so of course rather than say that, they ignored the whole matter and Robinson with it. And then, he had no "connections" to speak of, nor did he fit anyone's idea of what a poet should be like—an obscure hick living in obscurity, without influence, and with no capacity to push or dramatize himself. Nor did he belong to any literary coterie or movement which could do the pushing and dramatizing for him. The time did not allow for such. He was literally alone, and until poets ten to twenty years younger than he began to make themselves heard, after the Great War, he was absolutely alone on the American scene, though nobody knew except himself.

Captain Craig, although a youthful poem, is a highly conscious one. Robinson here explores at large a theme first adumbrated in "John Evereldown": Tilbury Town as materialistic America and vice versa. The Captain is of course our friend Alfred Louis, the apparent failure who has not failed but "merely not achieved." But more than that, the poem sets out to be an American poem, and in the well-worn passage in which the poet turns his irony against himself, his theme and America, he shows more forcefully than he could in a direct statement how conscious he was of being not just a poet but an American poet. The keynote of the poem is mockery—a mock-serious style, rising at times to eloquence, only to turn swiftly and deflate expansion before it can escape.

> Now you have read it through, and you know best
> What worth it has. We fellows with gray hair
> Who march with sticks to music that is gray
> Judge not your vanguard fifing. You are one
> To judge; and you will tell me what you think.
> Barring the Town, the Fair Maid, and the Feather,
> The dialogue and those parentheses,
> You cherish it, undoubtedly. 'Pardie'!
> You call it, with a few conservative
> Allowances, an excellent small thing
> For patient inexperience to do:
> Derivative, you say—still rather pretty.
> But what is wrong with Mr. Killegrew?
> Is he in love, or has he read Rossetti?—

The drawling, American tough-guy style, humorous, laconic, with touches of Mark Twain, Yankee deadpan and put-on culture, is reminiscent, or perhaps rather proleptic, of the modern academic who speaks bad grammar to undercut his learning. The poem is full of ironies and mild paradoxes and contrasts;

the blank verse swings along happily enough in an easy idiom
that can encompass colloquial humor, the mock-heroic, and the
truly Grand Style, all more or less crowding up against one
another.

> Now I call that as curious a dream
> As ever Meleager's mother had,—
> Eneas, Alcibiades or Jacob.
> I'll not except the scientist who dreamed
> That he was Adam and that he was Eve
> At the same time; or yet that other man
> Who dreamed that he was Aeschylus, reborn
> To clutch, combine, compensate and adjust
> The plunging and unfathomable chorus
> Wherein we catch, like a bacchanale through thunder,
> The chanting of the new Eumenides,
> Implacable, renascent, farcical,
> Triumphant, and American. He did it,
> But did it in a dream. When he awoke
> One phrase of it remained; one verse of it
> Went singing through the remnant of his life
> Like a bag-pipe in a mad-house.—He died young . . .

A modern reader may perhaps find rather less in it than Robinson
put there, partly because what was new then is old now and
there are other colloquial efforts in the modern mode that seem
to promise more. Nonetheless, *Captain Craig* reads well and easily
with no sense of strain on the part of the poet. If the Captain
himself grows a bit tedious, the narrator does not, nor does
so fine a comic invention as Count Pretzel Von Wurzburger,
the Obscene. Obviously this last must have been done from the
life, a composite of several types the poet knew in Coan's circle
or in the various lower West Side dives where he and his acquaintances spent their evenings. The most notable source of
inspiration for the character was one of the more curiously
sinister members of that long rogues' gallery that formed part
of Robinson's wide acquaintance, a grotesque named Joseph
Lewis French, whose career involved itself elaborately with
Robinson's. The man was by turns entrepreneur, amateur of
literature and the arts, critic and reviewer; first and foremost,

however, he attracted Robinson's interest by his combination of eccentricity, vitality and imagination. Yet the eccentricity could become morbid, the vitality threatening, the imagination insane. He did in fact die many years later in a sanitarium. All through Robinson's life there were the sudden irruptions of French, in his guise as mentor, panhandler, or threat. Robinson said more than once that he sometimes thought he would meet his death at French's hands, and there is no question but that certain friends took precautions to keep the two men apart. French often meant well, in his saner moments, and he loved Robinson's poetry, sufficient cause for forgiveness in the poet's eyes; indeed, French praised it in print, but one wonders what such auspices meant to readers and other poets. When all is said, however, French and Louis together make a pair of types in *Captain Craig* whose words and behavior give the poem some of its best moments, though readers may find Count Pretzel the more rewarding for the relative economy of the portrait. The whole poem smells of bohemianism and is meant to, since part of its charm derives from a youthful evocation of town types. The supposed locale is "Tilbury Town," the Gardiner of fact, but the provenience of the more notable characters is New York.

Reading *Captain Craig* along with the other poems in the volume gives us a sense of the degree of the poet's development up to this point. Some poems are in a Browningesque manner; others have that streak of melodrama I have noted; one or two explore what he himself called his "jingly vein" and which he later seemed rather to dislike—with reason, I think. But there are apart from the title poem at least two poems here to rank among his best, and one of them, "Isaac and Archibald," must stand as one of the great American poems. No American before this had written a blank verse so sinewy; no one would do it again till Stevens, in his very different voice, composed "Sunday Morning." There has been nothing since. The contrast between this poem and *Captain Craig* strikes one immediately: the latter shows an attractive, highly talented, original sensibility and imagination at work in a new but still tentative style and region. "Isaac and Archibald" is a masterwork, a small miracle of tone, control, speaking voice, and self-effacing description. The narrator's ironic and affectionate portrait of himself as a small boy,

of the two old men and of the very landscape of Maine on a
late summer day makes it a kind of American locus classicus;
it goes along with the very finest of Sarah Orne Jewett's stories.
Yet the poem does far more; critics often bring in Wordsworth,
and the parallels have validity, yet we look in vain for such
complexity of attitude in Wordsworth. No "egotistical sublime"
for Robinson and no irony for Wordsworth. The two poets
take very different routes to different ends. "Michael" cannot
admit humor, irony or relaxation; "Isaac and Archibald" evokes
and exploits those elements.

> Now and then my fancy caught
> A flying glimpse of a good life beyond—
> Something of ships and sunlight, streets and singing,
> Troy falling, and the ages coming back,
> And ages coming forward: Archibald
> And Isaac were good fellows in old clothes,
> And Agamemnon was a friend of mine;
> Ulysses coming home again to shoot
> With bows and feathered arrows made another,
> And all was as it should be. I was young.
>
> So I lay dreaming of what things I would,
> Calm and incorrigibly satisfied
> With apples and romance and ignorance
> And the still smoke from Archibald's clay pipe.
> There was a stillness over everything
> As if the spirit of heat had laid its hand
> Upon the world and hushed it; and I felt
> Within the mightiness of the white sun
> That smote the land around us and wrought out
> A fragrance from the trees, a vital warmth
> And fulness for the time that was to come,
> And a glory for the world beyond the forest.
> The present and the future and the past,
> Isaac and Archibald, the burning bush,
> The Trojans and the walls of Jericho,
> Were beautifully fused; and all went well
> Till Archibald began to fret for Isaac
> And said it was a master day for sunstroke.

What could easily inflate and then fall, what could turn sentimental, these Robinson holds firmly under control by the double
vision of the narrator: as boy and as the man recalling the boy's
adventure, with the result that we as readers can imagine boyhood, see its wonderful sensibility and its paradoxical failure
to understand. We have in a way a kind of Kennebec River
Huck Finn, who misreads most wonderfully what the grown man
can set right, but with none of the magic of incomprehension
only youth can give—or only youth-in-retrospect! Robinson must
have intended the poem as a kind of genre study, and like
anything in a particular mode that wholly succeeds, it transcends
its limits.

The other fine piece in the volume is "Aunt Imogen," a blank
verse narrative which all the Robinsonians see as an autobiographical portrait of the poet as maiden aunt, which is as it may
or may not be. Of course Robinson was adored by his small
nieces and returned their affection. In the poem he changes
names and sexes, but one can reasonably say that the poem is
"about" the poet's own realization that "there was no love /
Save borrowed love" for him, since he felt doomed to remain a
bachelor and Herman's children were all the family he had left.
Such interpretation may add poignancy, as if the poem needed
any more, but I suggest that Robinson knew about the matter
from other sources as well, and from one of these came another
of his great poems, "The Poor Relation." Like anyone growing
up in a New England town, he had seen the spinsters and
maiden ladies, the gentlewomen in reduced circumstances, the
pensioners as it were of more prosperous nephews, nieces, cousins,
the little old ladies who came in to do the sewing and upon
whom one had to call on holidays, birthdays and other state
and stated occasions. He knew full well what loneliness was
like; any man who does not is a clod. And he could imagine
the rest, particularly when he could see in the flesh those fading
or faded women whom marriage had passed by and whose
great gifts of love could be lavished only occasionally.

The poem is another study in time and place, though neither
is expressly given. No poet today would write about such a
thing, yet the thing still exists though we do not like to think
so. On this as on so many other subjects, Robinson wrote for

himself and for his own generation. Both "Aunt Imogen" and
"Isaac and Archibald" belong to his experience, his time and
place; he wrote them, put them down, to tell his own contemporaries what it was like, how it was. In this he resembles,
as in many other respects, his great near-contemporary Wallace
Stevens and his elder Yeats. "To write for my own race / And
the reality," as Yeats put it, might in this case become to write
for his own generation of Americans, northeastern subspecies.
For all the seeming generality and generalization of the poems,
they have roots in a particular time and town. If we look back
to Robinson's first venture in the longer poem, "The Night
Before," we can at once feel the difference. The events could
have taken place at any time, in any place where the melodramatic locale of a condemned cell would be a likelihood.
The very versification and meter of the poem show a crudeness
which evinces both the beginner and the experimentalist.

> Forgiveness! . . .
> What does it mean when the one forgiven
> Shivers and weeps and clings and kisses
> The credulous fool that holds her, and tells him
> A thousand things of a good man's mercy,
> And then slips off with a laugh and plunges
> Back to the sin she has quit for a season
> To tell him that hell and the world are better
> For her than a prophet's heaven?—Believe me,
> The love that dies ere its flames are wasted
> In search of an alien soul is better,
> Better by far than the lonely passion
> That burns back into the heart that feeds it.

Even in *Captain Craig,* a great advance on its predecessor, one
finds a flaccidity, a kind of catch-all randomness that shows the
young man feeling his powers but not yet wholly in charge. The
vision is in the process of becoming more concentrated and more
objective—but the poem still has too many private jokes and
chuckles, too many of the young man's pretensions and cultivated idiosyncracies. Both "Isaac and Archibald" and "Aunt
Imogen" surpass the former technically: the blank verse conveys meaning efficiently without ostentation but does not go

limp; the run-on lines carry meaning over and one has far less sense of syllable-counting. Above all, in each case meaning and verse conspire for particular effects. In "Aunt Imogen" the tone and the verse are single, quietly intense; the poet has a certain dramatic and emotional effect to get and he drives directly at it. Considerably shorter than "Isaac and Archibald," it might have gone the way of "The Night Before" as a piece of "spasmodic" poesy, accentuating the emotional pathetic at the expense of intensity and quiet. I cannot believe that "The Night Before" did not derive much from Tennyson and *Maud,* but where the latter shows Tennyson as the mature, powerful experimenter in both metric and expressive possibilities, and manipulates several tones throughout as well as symbolic patterns, Robinson's poem simply stakes all on a melodramatic plot, which has neither originality nor relevance to real experience.

Robinson must have recognized his own "spasmodic" tendencies. Though he wrote many poems in which the plot, so to speak, turns on an act of violence, he admitted in individual cases that he had not succeeded—in the case of "The Whip," for example. He is by no means the first poet to write against his best grain, as though what we consider his failures alone made possible the successes. In this book, *The Children of the Night,* the best of his gift shines in at least two poems; touches of his finest lesser mastery show in "The Field of Glory," and I think personally that in "The Book of Annandale" we meet again our "spasmodic" poet, the melodramatist and perhaps obscurantist. The poem begins well: inevitably it reminds us of "Reuben Bright" and the Tilbury Town poems, but it lacks roots, and instead of moving, going and getting somewhere, it seeps away underground, so to speak, and tries to elicit from mystification an element of suspense and excitement. But worst of all, the rhetoric. Beginning with a good, tight muscular style, it loses its way and then simply goes to pieces rhetorically, most notably in the description, given through the awareness of Damaris, of Annandale's "book" and language.

> Yes, like an anodyne the voice of him,
> There were the words that he had made for her,
> For her alone. The more she thought of them

The more she lived them, and the more she knew
The life-grip and the pulse of warm strength in them.
They were the first and last of words to her,
And there was in them a far questioning
That had for long been variously at work,
Divinely and elusively at work,
With her, and with the grave that had been hers;
They were eternal words, and they diffused
A flame of meaning that men's lexicons
Had never kindled; they were choral words
That harmonized with love's enduring chords
Like wisdom with release; triumphant words
That rang like elemental orisons
Through ages out of ages; words that fed
Love's hunger in the spirit; words that smote;
Thrilled words that echoed, and barbed words that clung;—

The entire passage is too long and bad to set down here; what I would suggest to the reader is that Robinson often, in blank verse narrative, lost interest, or his way, and kept on writing in the hope that something would turn up. To put it bluntly, the writing is lazy and self-indulgent. Easy writing, as Byron remarked, makes cursed hard reading. And finally on this subject, the matter of reference and comparison. Now from time to time Robinson's trick of comparing one action to another wholly differently located or constituted, of equating, ironically, the simple with the complex, and vice versa, has validity and wit. But all too frequently he seemed to enjoy such tricks too much and indeed they become a kind of "tic douloureux." The opening lines of *Captain Craig* provide an instance of what I mean when the narrator says that folk in Tilbury Town had never looked at the Captain "So curiously or so concernedly / As they had looked at ashes . . ." Mildly amusing and wholly appropriate to the tone of the poem and its theme. Moreover, as I have suggested, the poem deals in various voices and rhetorics; immature in some ways though it may be, it has youthful vitality, ebullience and unexpectedness. We can see Robinson enjoying his powers, and on the whole we enjoy them along with him. When he gives us a Robinsonian compari-

son such as "My friends got out / Like brokers out of Arcady"
we can provide the dimension he asks, of mild wit and the less
mild irony, and similarly, when he indulges in a rhetorical set
piece like the famous passage describing "that other man /
Who dreamed that he was Aeschylus, reborn . . ." Robinson
piles it on deliberately, in part from a motive of real furor
poeticus and yet, equally deliberately, with the ironic awareness
that the man is a dreamer and his aim chimerical. Here his
choice of conflicting adjectives indicates that the poet sees himself as at once deluded and conscious of it, hefting his self-
imposed burden, yet convinced that perhaps, with luck and good
management, he may be able to bear it after all and turn dream
to actuality. "Implacable, renascent, farcical, / Triumphant,
and American . . ." The entire passage might serve as apologia,
manifesto, or valedictory.

"The Book of Annandale" lacks anything of the wit, verve,
humanity and size of *Captain Craig*. Robinson gives us the situation quickly and efficiently, albeit vaguely. As we move along,
it becomes apparent, I think, that here we have one of Robinson's Jamesian narratives, in this case his version of "The Beast
in the Jungle," for Annandale seems to be a man who has felt
nothing truly, and the poem catches him, just after his wife's
death, in the act of discovering that he has never really loved
her:

> . . . there came
> No clearer meaning to him than had come
> Before: the old abstraction was the best
> That he could find, the farthest he could go . . .

Both Annandale and Damaris, "the other woman," have in
reality mistaken both their lives and their loves. The "book" of
Annandale in effect has liberated Damaris from her bondage to
the "ghost" of her dead husband, as it has set the stage for
Annandale to recognize Damaris as his true love, the one for
whom he wrote his book, though he did not know it. The story
is one of recognition, revelation, reconciliation, with certain
elements of deliberate mystification; Robinson here, as often
elsewhere, likes to withhold certain information in order to
achieve a kind of suspense, just as he likes to qualify and split

hairs to the point of incomprehensibility. Aiming, in this poem, for a climax, a moment of revelation when Damaris realizes that she has been set free, that both Annandale and his "book" are for her, Robinson has recourse to a vague and periphrastic rhetoric that simply robs the poem of force and conviction. For Robinson in this poem, as in many of the other narratives, the question is, How to go beyond "the old abstraction." He comes very near to doing it in *Amaranth,* I think; in *Captain Craig,* "Isaac and Archibald" and "Aunt Imogen" he avoids the abstract, or at any rate finds witty, ironic and sometimes very particular ways to make his abstractions real, tangible. One need not labor the symbolic significance of the fine passage in "Isaac" when the two old men and the boy go down into the cellar to sample Archibald's cider. It is finely realized in the full sense of the word, rooted in the actual, in memory, in a place and time Robinson could no more fail to respond to than he could fail, responding so, to capture it. Imagination doing its best and proper work, no work of the will and the Meredithian intellect, and worth more than all the abstractions another approach to the theme might have spawned. But memory holds the key in this instance as in so many others. Occasionally in a narrative of medium length he could capture the essence of a spiritual dilemma or crisis and by projecting his own crises into an imagined or historical figure, could "clutch, combine, compensate and adjust" that figure and his own experience, to compose a tertium quid: a Robinsonian artist-hero, like his Shakespeare of "Ben Jonson Entertains a Man from Stratford," or that most Robinsonian of Hollanders in "Rembrandt to Rembrandt." As always, the point is that Robinson uses the historical "fact" or the objective, realistic, intractable "story" as a way to reach the subjective, the almost autobiographical. Where another poet might use symbol, he uses exemplary characters, situations, plights. Captain Craig as character, hero, myth and symbol: Robinson staked his all as a mature poet on the volume that bears the Captain's name; a flawed, but impressive performance absolutely beyond the reach of anyone else writing in America or Britain at that time. He might as well have saved his energy. But of course he would not have, even had he foreseen.

In Jimmie Moore's old rundown brownstone at 450 West

23rd Street, the poet found a home in these days. Moore seems to have been a convivial, riotous, boon companion who, along with his brother who ran a bar uptown, played host to the bohemia of the Village and its purlieus. No one knew or cared who came home with whom; the house must have been bedlam many nights, with all-night parties, sudden irruptions of the constabulary and evictions of young women in varied conditions. A most irregular life for a poet like Robinson, yet he was never one to cast stones, either first or last, and apparently looked on the sexual lives of his acquaintances as something at times inconvenient but by no means wicked. Jimmie Moore gave Robinson the room he occupied rent-free, or next thing to it, and there he lived, withdrawn, remote. He touched on the one hand the world of the down-and-out, on the other, that of Bohemia and art. His circle of friends included Burnham and Saben from his Harvard days; the former moved into Jimmie Moore's and the two friends remained close. Robinson had got to know the sculptor James Earle Fraser as well as certain other minor poets of the period, such as Ridgely Torrence, who would after EA's death edit a collection of his letters; and in Boston, Josephine Preston Peabody, whom he always saw when he visited Boston and with whom he corresponded for some years. And then there were the curious hangers-on of the sort he had met at Coan's house in 1898–99, most notable or notorious among them being Joseph Lewis French, the original of Count Pretzel in *Captain Craig*. There were a good many others, and it almost seems as though anyone who ever knew Robinson never allowed him to drop completely out of sight or mind. Some of them, like Jimmie Barstow, found him work; others, like Edmund Clarence Stedman, the anthologist-stockbroker who had a bad case of poetitis, tried to push him in various quarters of publishing. But the real trouble was that this poet wouldn't work, except on poetry. By the time it became clear that *Captain Craig* had not even ruffled the surface of literary politics, Robinson was down and very near to despair.

To add to the misery of unsuccess and penury came periodic news from the House on Lincoln Avenue, Gardiner. Herman, by now little more than a drunk, had moved out, and what he, his wife and children would live on remained a question. For at least part of the time Herman seems to have lived in the summer cottage on Capitol Island, near Boothbay Harbor, which he had built but could not pay for, thus allowing the property to go to Emma's parents. The poet himself could do little or nothing, but as soon as fate in the form of Theodore Roosevelt intervened, he began sending money home and did so faithfully and increasingly till his death. But meantime he had to eat—and just as important, drink. Liquor. We must bear in mind that ever since *Lippincott's Magazine* had accepted and paid for his sonnet on Poe in 1893 (and did not print it for twelve years) he had made not one cent from poetry, nor had he even so much as appeared in the better literary magazines. Not only would they return his poems, but one editor peremptorily forbade him to send him any more. I rather suspect that today, in similar case, a poet might have resort to paranoia; Robinson simply withdrew and stopped writing. In effect he lost courage and almost his identity. He reached the nadir with a job in the subway, going home from long, damp dismal hours underground to drink himself stupid and fall asleep. His friends could do nothing, if they knew, and the ones who might have done something were too far away to know and Robinson never let on how bad it was with him. If by 1905 Theodore Roosevelt with his patronage had lifted him up and placed him in the light again, nonetheless irreparable damage had been done, which is not to say that life is not a damaging business at best, but only that most of us would prefer, if we have to be killed, to be killed with kindness. These years between his first book and 1905, when he was only thirty-six, killed his youth and ebullience unnecessarily soon and quickly. The somber, unrelieved tones of his work deepened, and indeed for a time he stopped writing altogether. Friends kept him going, friends and drink, and both of them together, fortunately. Late in the evening, after hours of cruising the West Side bars with friends such as Torrence, his eye would light up, his tongue loosen and his spirits would, if not soar, at least lift. Then there was good talk and lots of it. But he could not of course live that way for long; in the first place it took a great deal of whiskey to get him to that stage and it incapacitated him the next day. Roosevelt's help came none too soon. Though it did not encourage Robinson to work, and though the President's patronage really gained him more hostility than favor among editors and the literary politicians, it gave him a new hold on his self-respect.

In that same year he moved from Jimmie Moore's to the Judson on Washington Square, then and for some time to come a hotel for writers and artists of all kinds. Frank Norris lived there for a time, and of course Moody, and two other poets who would become his friends, Louis Ledoux and Percy MacKaye, came in and out. And here there occurred one of those events that one would have given much to have observed: Isadora Duncan's attempt, wholly unsuccessful, to seduce the adamant and apparently unembarrassed Robinson. Yet he was in grave danger of cutting himself off from people and from his art. Stedman and others whom he had once visited knew him no more; no one seemed able to shift him, to get him out of his room or himself, except when night came and he would go the rounds of the bars.

When did he write? For the most part, he got up late, went down to the Customs House for a time and read the papers, then back to the hotel till dinner and drinking time. He did not write for a long time—perhaps for three or even four years he may have written next to nothing, in verse at least. For much of this time he broke himself, like Henry James before him and many another since, on the rack of the theater, trying to make his way into fame and fortune and meeting failure again. Two plays, *Van Zorn* and *The Porcupine,* survive in print from the period. Moody's success with *The Great Divide* and MacKaye's and Josephine Peabody's enthusiasm over what they felt was a new era in American theater, proved contagious. The dramatic revival abroad, the hope for a kind of Elizabethan age in America, the periodic sensation that now is the time, Broadway will yet see the light, poets will proclaim a new dawn of drama and Philistia will fall: all these enthusiasms filled the air. To Robinson, however, who liked the theater—almost any theater—the drama pointed towards success and money. He needed both, particularly the latter, and primarily to help his sister-in-law and his nieces. When he failed as a playwright, his gloom thickened, and of course poetry got harder and harder even to think of, let alone write.

Some of his friends thought alcohol was the problem. Clearly, they mistook him; alcohol worked beneficently on him. It got him through the grim winter of the subway and now stood between him and despair. But he could not go on like that much longer. In the spring of 1909, Roosevelt left office, Taft came in, and Robinson lost his job because he was now asked to put in a day's work. Starve he might, but *work* for the Customs? He simply quit.

When he went back to Gardiner that fall, he found changes. His brother Herman had died in a ward of the Boston City Hospital the winter before, alone, alcoholic, down and out. Emma had to sell the house on Lincoln Avenue and move to her parents' house in Farmingdale with her three daughters, but they had survived, and chiefly because EA had used the money from his job in the Customs House to ensure that survival. And back in Gardiner he began to write poems again. He had never found New York a place to write in. He loved it, loved living there and had the feel of it as no other poet except Hart Crane has, but he could never do much writing there and came to realize the fact surprisingly late. In this fall of 1909 his pent-up poetic energy made its demand. A sudden order came into his life. There with his sister-in-law and the girls to steady him, with the familiar landscape around him, he wrote. No more alcohol now, but the loving companionship of his nieces and long evenings with Emma. If he had ever really loved Emma with anything more than a young boy's romantic yearning, now would have been the time to declare. Chard Powers Smith puts forward theory and proof in the form of selected passages from the poems, but that kind of game any theoretician or indeed fanatic can play. We do know that his nieces did not and do not believe their mother loved any man except their father, and at this time when Ruth was eighteen, the most infatuated of nieces would have observed it if "Uncle Win" and Mother had been lovers or in love. The matter would not really merit discussion except that once dragged in, it has to be dealt with. The trauma Robinson suffered from all his life— if it was a trauma and it was that from which he suffered— cannot have been love. "Men have died and worms have eaten them, but not for love." Or any other selected animadversion.

He suffered from practically everything but mostly from being alive and a poet in a world he never made. The years since the absolute failure of *Captain Craig* found him exhausted. The work of his youth and young manhood was over; he had failed to win an audience for his poetry and to make a living. He had gone down to the bottom and survived. He had to come back up, and when he did he would be in a sense born again. That very theme would dominate in the poems he would write thereafter.

The Town Down the River appeared, if that is the word, in 1910. Robinson was trying to protect himself from adverse criticism and from total neglect by making the usual self-deprecatory remarks, but in fact he expected great things of the book and he dedicated it to Theodore Roosevelt—a kind of *quid pro quo,* just as he used to give manuscripts to friends who loaned him money. It got a patronizing comment in the New York *Times,* but in the Boston *Transcript* William Stanley Braithwaite gave it an intelligent and laudatory notice, on the strength of which Robinson looked up his admirer and they became friends. Robinson meant what he had often said: that if one disliked his poetry one disliked him because the poetry was the best of him. In *The Town Down the River* some of the best of the poetry shines out. Exactly when he wrote it we cannot know, but a few poems must have been written over the long eight years in New York after *Captain Craig,* though we can be sure that "The Island" was written in Gardiner in the fall of 1909 and can safely assume that the months after his return there brought most of the poems to light. Some few might have been early ones reworked, but the sudden burst of energy from September till spring, 1909–10, would appear to account for the preponderance of the work. We might note that in this book there are more Tilbury Town, as well as New York, poems than in *Captain Craig,* which may suggest that the poet's experience of New York not only had helped to distance his view of Gardiner, but also that the return to Gardiner allowed him to make his New York experience into poems and to rediscover Tilbury Town, for poetic purposes. Indeed, for the first time, really, at least in the short pieces, the town fully captures his imagination, and the characters who emerge find their places in Tilbury Town, no matter what their actual provenience. By the same token, New York begins to attract to it odd characters and types who have their poetic lives there though they may not belong to the scene at all. The very title of the book suggests a neat double irony, typical of Robinson humor. The "town" is New York. Down the river from that other town, Gardiner. The poles, antipodes, extremes of the native American talent. From rags to riches and back again, from hick to slicker and return. It is not, of course, that the sounds and sights and smells of either place figure much in any poem; there is nothing like "Isaac and Archibald" here. But for one thing, we find a number of poems about people or events or both that somehow manage to suggest the place and milieu appropriate to each, as for example, "Doctor of Billiards" suggests a New York pool parlor, "Calverly's" one of the many bars of the West Side the poet knew well. And many come directly from experiences we know of, or deal with people whom we can identify: "Miniver Cheevy" is a sardonic self-portrait, "For a Dead Lady" has to do with Mary Robinson, "Pasa Thalassa Thalassa" with Captain Jordan, the father of childhood friends and neighbors, just as "Lingard and the Stars" derives from the poet's experience with table-tipping years before, "The White Lights" celebrates the successful opening of Moody's *The Great Divide,* and "For Arvia" addresses his niece. Still others seem to have autobiographical tones, which does not so much provide the occasion or excuse for detective work as it suggests how Robinson had, over the past few years, found his own "usable past" and how he could turn personal experience into the four-dimensional object that is a successful poem.

This book has its share of undistinguished verses, but most succeed, though a number are unpretentious and seem like exercises for greater work to come. I think "The Island" is the least attractive of the volume as it is by far the longest, and some of the work strikes one as a little thin, almost tired, as well it might have been. "Leonora" and "Pasa Thalassa Thalassa," in what he called his "jingly vein," have a Kiplingesque quality that is derivative, fin de siècle and, though most competent, uninspired. I should guess they belong to an earlier period and were reworked. And there are at least two of Robinson's "trick" poems, poems with, as it were, O. Henry plots: "The Whip" and "How Annandale Went Out." They look back to "Richard Cory" and, happily, ahead to "The Mill," the one wholly successful, indeed masterly, piece in this genre; unlike others, it is rooted in circumstance and wholly escapes melodrama.

But in this book we find at least two superb poems, "For a Dead Lady" and "Two Gardens in Linndale." They differ widely in tone, subject matter, fundamental attitude, and they show Robinson at his or anyone else's best in that time. Half a dozen or more others repay repeated reading, notably "Momus," "Exit," "Alma Mater," "The Companion," "The Master," "The White Lights"—just listing them suggests still more. On the whole, however, the two greatest stand clearly above these others, fine though they are, and it is necessary for us, if only to base an admiration for Robinson's work more firmly on as full an understanding as analysis can provide, to look at these two poems, for what they are and for the exemplary purpose they fulfill.

"For a Dead Lady" certainly deals with Mary Palmer Robinson and may well deal with her son Edwin. Whatever we may think of the thesis that practically all Robinson's work touches in some way on Herman, Emma, EA and their remarkable imputed relationships, one cannot ignore the regular recurrence in the poetry of the success that turns to failure and the insignificance that assumes great importance. But a desire to find "the figure in the carpet" all too frequently leads to reductive criticism, a simplistic and unimaginative urge to lump all elements together under a single rubric. "Two Gardens in Linndale" defies such a method by dealing with a theme we ordinarily do not associate with Robinson, and by maintaining a tone and a balance to be found rarely in poetry of this gentle, mocking, tough and masculine sort. The poem is about art, about poetry. Robinson would have agreed with Kipling that "There are nine and sixty ways / of constructing tribal lays / And every single one of them is right." But he had his ways which were not those of his contemporaries nor those of his successors, and those ways had to be right—for him; hence the self-deprecating insight, with its double-edged irony, of his retort when asked if he wrote free verse: "No, I write badly enough as it is." I enter here a caveat: like Eliot's Sweeney, "I gotta use words when I talk to you" and the words can mislead. I do not mean to suggest that the poem under discussion is solely or even primarily about poetry; I do suggest—indeed I strongly feel—that "poetry" here becomes a symbol of man's devotion to a great endeavor impossible of achievement, one which uplifts him as man and brings him close to both his forebears and his brothers, and in so doing creates a grace beyond the reach of art.

The framework of action, the "plot" as it were, has to do with the two brothers, Oakes and Oliver, who have inherited land from their father and proceed, in good New England fashion, to divide it equally between them and to fence off each portion from the other, for the reason that each has his own particular form of gardening to do and wishes to go about it as best he can while not interfering with his brother's desires. Oakes will raise artichokes, Oliver the conventional and certain crops. Year after year each works at his garden and just as regularly Oakes's crop fails, till at last he dies and "the land was all for Oliver." The brothers differ greatly in all but their gentleness and their affection for one another; the poem may in some sense represent Robinson's view of the life of art and the relativity of success in life and in one's work, notably imaginative work. In the background is the "Linndale, where their fathers died," as there remain always immanent the "Paradise," the "Stranger," and the "garden." One hesitates to speak of allegory, but perhaps we might call the poem a species of exemplary and symbolic narrative.

Look first at technique, as craft. Robinson always got his best effects in the tightly knit stanza with lines of from short to medium length, rhyming closely and sharply, often with alternating masculine and feminine endings. There are exceptions of course and I do not at this point include any reference to the poems in blank verse. In the poem of from three to thirty stanzas he gets his finest effects, primarily by quickly establishing a seemingly dry, efficient, ironic tone which allows him to efface himself as narrator while he manipulates our responses by varying the tone ever so slightly by subtly unobtrusive means. Further, the technique gives him opportunities for wit and humor, again a humor deriving from a subtly varied tone, as we see in " 'Divine!' said Oakes," or in the fine phrase "like amateurs in paradise" with its clear pun and its suggestion of the absurd yet triumphant. The two brothers are indeed unfallen men: Oakes says that he finds in Oliver "as fair a thing indeed / As ever bloomed and ran to seed / Since Adam was a gardener." In their incorrigible innocence, these two men cultivate the impossible—or rather, Oakes does while Oliver, "the gentle anchorite," encourages his brother in his impossible but not hopeless task and himself believing, if not in Oakes's ultimate success, certainly in Oakes, which amounts perhaps to more in the long run.

Oakes has "the vision and the voice" and, after his death, Oliver thinks and speculates alone by his grave on the visionary who was his brother, and at dawn listens for the voices Oakes can no longer hear.

> He cannot sing without the voice
> But he may worship and rejoice
> For patience in him to remain,
> The chosen heir of age and pain,
> Instead of Oakes—who had no choice.

Earlier in the poem Oakes has said that if each is right in his own way, they shall both "sing together such a song / As no man yet sings anywhere." Both men before the fall, they enjoy God's grace to the full, and as Oliver sits at evening wondering "what new race / Will have two gardens, by God's grace," he imagines his dead brother in some Elysian field "uprooting, with a restless hand / Soft shadowy flowers in a land / Of asphodels and artichokes."

The poem is as neatly put together as any neo-Metaphysical exercise of the Eliot–Ransom period, but it achieves tenderness without going coy or arch, and resilience and toughness without flexing muscles. Above all, it is not literary in the pedantic or "knowing" senses of the word. It deals in ambiguities (What about that "fence"? Who's mending the wall?). How far shall we push the notions of "grace"? of the Adamic? of "vision" and "voice"? Everything is oddly familiar, with emphasis upon the odd, since Robinson has created an atmosphere of timelessness where these two innocents can labor and sing and hope and enjoy—"till on a day the Stranger came." Whether Oakes has the "vision and the voice" or not, death will come even to this near-paradise, which can be only so near. Oakes has said that they are "in tune with Fate" and of course that "one season longer will suffice." Most ironically, it does: time runs out, Fate breaks off the tune, death comes and in a stanza of the simplest elegance the narrator tells us what happens:

> He came to greet them where they were
> And he too was a Gardener:
> He stood between these gentle men,
> He stayed a little while, and then
> The land was all for Oliver.

The land was left them by their "fathers"; they divided it between them, and now Oliver owns it all, while he wonders who will inherit it from him. No one, perhaps. As is so often the case with a Robinson poem, the question remains open, not so much that we may solve a problem to our own satisfaction as to suggest that the point is neither to solve nor to put a problem, but to create a kind of model of a general sort of human involvement—and involvement with others, with a "vision," with mortality. All this is only to say that Robinsonian irony almost never destroys; it heals and comforts as it contemplates the incomprehensible or the catastrophic. Such poems compare to fields of force in which many energetic possibilities move from an interior state to an external and realize themselves in the persons and actions of the poems but also as poetic actions both complete in themselves yet opening out, moving like energy itself, forever escaping.

"For a Dead Lady" has the same qualities of an example or "model." Though utterly different in tone from "Two Gardens," it has comparable movement, technique and range. The classic Robinsonian form: alternate masculine and feminine rhymes with the barest minimum of running-on thereby making us come down sharply on the rhyme words. Only in the last of the three stanzas do we find considerable running-on: with a hesitant faltering in the first four lines, then with a powerful, almost denunciatory sweep in the final four. Again and again in Robinson's lyrics, one sees how much he can get from a small tech-

nical effect; he doesn't need to resort to what Wordsworth
called "gross stimulants" to get our attention and keep it. Just
when we may be about to find the technique verging on the
mechanical, he gives it a flick, a fillip, and suddenly everything
is transformed.

> No more with overflowing light
> Shall fill the eyes that now are faded
> Nor shall another's fringe with night
> Their woman-hidden world as they did.
> No more shall quiver down the days
> The flowing wonder of her ways,
> Whereof no language may requite
> The shifting and the many-shaded.

Take, for example, the counterpointed rhythm in line three of
the first stanza; the opening two lines, wholly regular, are succeeded by a line in which the stress is forced down on "nor"
and taken off "shall" where we would normally expect it. With
the pulled-out "another's" following this inversion, we get a
sense of wrenching, of unsettling effective in itself as well as
indicative of the most unsettling attitude the poem will finally
adopt. Again, take the first example in the poem of enjamb-
ment: we run directly over, in line three of the second stanza,
to the phrase "is hushed," there is a pause, then comes the
desolate "and answers to no calling." Finally, consider how in
the final line of the poem Robinson strikes the first four syl-
lables with firm but not heavy strokes: the adjective "vicious"
fairly leaps out, takes on a meaning far beyond what we might
expect of the word. And I take that to be one test at least of
a poet's power and mastery.

> And we who delve in beauty's lore
> Know all that we have known before
> Of what inexorable cause
> Makes Time so vicious in his reaping.

The poem is neither as subtle in theme nor as complex in
development as "Two Gardens": it is not intended to be. What
we have here is a totally objectified cry of individual pain.
The poem neither protests nor defies. It does not "curse God

and die," a line from Job which Robinson would later appropriate for "The Man Against the Sky." It *presents*. This is how it
is, we are told. The notion is akin to that expressed in "The
Clerks," where poets and kings are as much slaves of Time—
which to Robinson is Fate in another guise—as "we who delve
in beauty's lore" are, and must remain ignorant of whatever
force of hap, to use Hardy's word, causes or simply allows
gratuitous pain.

Robinson is a deceptively simple technician and thinker-poet.
He does not come on strong with the culture and the allusions
and the pedantry and the esoteric that so many of those who
followed after would provide. He has often been likened to
Browning, a comparison he almost violently rejected, and properly: Eliot and Pound owe far more to Browning than he does,
and the Browning influence that permeated the twenties seems
today the more remarkable because those who most felt it most
fully rejected their Victorian forebears. Robinson was a Victorian in many senses, but he broke with its esthetics long before Pound began to refurbish it for modern use. The irony of
the phrase "beauty's lore" was not lost on Robinson though it
has been on many critics. "Beauty's lore" indeed! Had he not
from the beginning spewed the word beauty out of his mouth?
But he deals in hints and suggestion which readers frequently
do not take because they have not caught the tone—a tone of
mockery sometimes, of self-deprecation, of straightforwardness
masking subtlety. In "For a Dead Lady" I suggest that common
words are being used in most uncommon ways, that subtle
hints and forewarnings-and-shadowings tease us on through the
poem and prepare us for the shattering conclusion. We did not
expect all this—but we might have known! Consider first in the
first stanza the following words: woman-hidden, quiver, flowing,
shifting, many-shaded. Isolated thus, they suddenly show their
kinship and purpose: they have been put there to tell us some
very particular things but in ways that we won't recognize until
the end, if then or at all. I hasten to add that the recognition is, if not irrelevant, supererogatory: it won't save your soul.
I am concerned with Robinson's technique, his craft if you like,
and no one has had a finer, excepting only Stevens in his very
different way, in the twentieth century. Robinson does not have

to recognize or know why he used those words; a lifetime of training taught him to know that they worked as put down there where they still are, and I take it that is what technique means: knowing how and doing it.

What do those words do? For one thing, they show how ambiguous the lady appears to us and how equivocal the poet's reaction to her becomes. "The laugh that love could not forgive" in stanza two would surely be unforgivable, technically, had those other words not prepared for it. The lady is like water, like light and shade, like "overflowing light"—and so are the poet's reactions to her. I do not most particularly mean anything Freudian here. Cannot a man love his mother and yet know that she not only had faults but that she did not love him as much as he did her? A fact of life we all know; there are the lovers and the ones who let themselves be loved. Mothers are no exception. Robinson does not go on about that; he just, just barely, raises the point, then lets it sink back below the surface. We do not need to go to Robinson's life and the horror of Mary Robinson's death to decorate the poem with neo-Gothic; it isn't about the horror of that personal death but about what Poe said was the sure-fire subject for poems: the death of a beautiful woman. When Robinson says "beauty's lore" he means the study of an abstract, aesthetic ideal without either relevance or materiality. What is that to Time's vicious and wholly inscrutable killing? In the face of such an insight, can we, he seems to ask, put any faith in ideals of beauty, truth and goodness? Was she not good, beautiful and true?

The particularity of the single case. The field of force or energy that case engenders. The opening out, release, escape of that energy. "For a Dead Lady" in its very title puts the case: a lady—not just a woman—has died. The poem does not touch on the manner and causes of her death, nor does the poet express sorrow or pain. He emphasizes in the first stanza the lady's grace and various charm; in the second he states that the lady's beauty has disappeared with her life, though perhaps the remembrance of her is not one of total idealization; in stanza three the beauty of the lady, now broken, becomes all beauty and must not simply die but wholly disappear, and perhaps by most horrible means. Yeats's "man is in love and loves what vanishes / What more is there to say?" comes very strongly to mind in this context. Robinson, like Yeats in so many poems that deal with loss and death, begins with the particular and allows the poem to open out at the last, so that it becomes a comment on time, mutability, love, art.

"For A Dead Lady" has great complexity, and one might succumb to the temptation to analyze it down to the last feminine ending. Yet despite the flattery of the poet such a procedure might imply, I cannot think many poets would find it genuinely laudatory. Exhaustiveness and exhaustion tend to merge in such cases; critics may say, with some small justice, that analysis never hurt anything good, but since it is their own métier which they would vindicate, the reader should feel free to preserve his scepticism. After all, it is an axiom of the law that no man is to be trusted in the pleading of his own cause, and critics, particularly when they mask self-interest with rationality, can do and have done damage to readers and to poems; they have as it were to the marriage of true minds admitted and enforced impediments. Yet some measure of understanding depends on a graspable meaning, and to find meaning we must find the approach to it. Poetry has many kinds of possible meanings and approaches, and what works for Donne will not do for Ben Jonson, as the New Critics demonstrate. John Crowe Ransom tries to get at the sonnets of Shakespeare by means of a technique especially developed in the laboratories of the New Criticism for the examination of Metaphysical verse—and repels the very object of his scrutiny by the rumor of his approach with the result that he is left with his own predilection: Donne is better than Shakespeare. As a judgment, interesting for the light it sheds on the judge and his mind; as criticism, it has neither value nor charm and can only mislead or deceive those who have read neither poet. By the same token, Miss Susan Sontag, who seeks the opposite pole, finds all "interpretation" worthless and even more than that, square. Disciple of the technocrats of the "nouvelle roman," apostle of entropy and practically pre-Gutenberg, she sees a work of literature as a happening described, without past and going nowhere, simply a kind of contraceptive device of the moment.

I do not use these two eminences as whipping boy or girl;

I simply use them as points of reference. Criticism has today assumed the function of an autotelic, self-referential art, and indeed many critics, like Norman Podhoretz, have abandoned the novel as an object of scrutiny and would elevate the critical endeavor to the rank of "the supreme fiction." Too bad. Can anyone deny that any kind of writing presents difficulties? That to criticize truly and sensibly demands great powers and great humility? And can we deny that today most criticism exalts itself (when it is not mere puffery) at the expense of what it purports to criticize? I suggest at this point, and in the case of Robinson, that we need to devise techniques of discussion which have not been so misused as to be suspect, or so neologistic and imprecise as to have achieved meaninglessness. Common sense may not seem to most of us the key to a discussion of a poem, but the finest critical minds have gone astray when they leave good sense. Samuel Johnson remains the finest critic in English because, for all his faults, he aimed always at sense and tried always to relate the personal and the communal. For him as for Robinson, the civilized man and woman count more than anything else, because without them there is nothing. The wildness of the human heart, the terror of the world, the universe, have power to move but not shake only those spirits who know the worst in advance and who, though they both bend and break, still believe that despair is no man's part, for all they understand and pity men in despair. Civilize, civilize—and remember that the wilderness is nearest when we think it farthest. In our time literature and criticism which foster such aims have not been popular; indeed, many critics specifically denounce them. George Steiner, for example, if he is a critic, demands that we recognize the implications of Buchenwald and that in the light of such horrors we can only disappear into silence. But such counsel is idle: we live here and now. Horror is man's condition, as it is his duty to resist horror and, where he can, wipe out the infamy. Poetry of the sort Robinson wrote knows a good deal about horror and infamy, and on a scale we small men can grasp. Great crimes against humanity, catastrophes engineered by stupid, willful and self-seeking men, or by outright maniacs, these may be the object of the poet's thought, and they may not. To turn from art because it will not flatter us in our fantasies of guilt or monstrousness or whatever, is the final betrayal. Criticism is bankrupt because it has reached total solipsism, because the critics themselves do not like what they purport to criticize, because they lack belief in the reality of literature. No wonder they do not know how to approach a poetry such as Robinson's. For him people exist. As Robert Penn Warren has it, "The world is real, it is there."

After the fall of 1909, Robinson returned to New York from Gardiner, there to occupy a studio at 121 Washington Place built for him by a Mrs. Clara Davidge, a lion-huntress whom Torrence had undertaken to guide to her prey. She was among the first of many ladies of a certain age and condition who later populated Robinson country. Not as bad a case as Browning's, by a long shot, but bad enough. Apparently, though, Mrs. Davidge's studio and whatever other amenities may have been laid on did not quite do, because the rhythm of his writing remained the same: he wrote, not in New York but in Boston, Gardiner, any other place that might suit. In New York he lived and drank and invited his soul and the souls of a few others. He left Washington Place for Chocorua, New Hampshire, where he lived with one of those semiderelicts and demigeniuses, like French, who seemed to be as attracted to Robinson as ladies of a certain age and condition. This character, Truman H. Bartlett, whom he had known in his Boston days, was of a piece with French, Alfred Louis and others, composite versions of whom we may read in *Captain Craig*, "The Wandering Jew," "Old Trails" and in bits and pieces here and there in many other poems. There, looking out at Mount Chocorua, he set to work to write something for money—not plays this time but fiction. He had a number of years before—right after his return home from Harvard—written a number of short stories. The epigraph from Coppée that opened his first book, and his many references to Daudet, showed then that he had always read and admired certain kinds of fiction. Henry James and George Meredith he admired greatly, and there were others less illustrious, though Hawthorne remained his favorite among the Americans. But none of his early stories survive; apparently he destroyed them all, in revulsion when his scheme of finding fame and fortune collapsed. Now in Chocorua in 1910 he aimed at a novel—or perhaps novels—beginning with an attempt at turning his play *Van Zorn* into fiction. He had written to Betts the previous summer that he had "fled" New York. He had to write; to risk another long silence might be dangerous, perhaps. But in New Hampshire there were other dangers. He wrote further to Betts that he hoped soon to "be more at ease with nature. This place is a heavy dose for a neophyte but I see that I am going to like it. My only fear is that I may like it too well . . ." He did not foresee that soon he would begin dividing his life between New Hampshire and New York, the old rhythm of *rus in urbe, urbs in rure* that seems always to have been a part of his nature even before he knew what city life was like or truly "saw" nature as the place where he lived.

Life in such isolation with the curious Bartlett for sole companion might have finished another man; it worked for Robinson. Though he got on Bartlett's nerves and Bartlett on his, still, they made it through till the snows came to stay, when Robinson left for New York and Mrs. Davidge's lion's cage on Washington Place. *The Town Down the River* had just come out, another book of poems which, for all he could tell, had fallen into limbo along with its predecessors. He went on writing his fiction. For a full three years he wrote and wrote and sold nothing. Poetry he seemed to have abandoned. He wanted money, the fame that goes with enough of it, and he wanted to be able to support both himself and his nieces and their mother. His friends must have known that he was in a bad way, drinking hard, and writing not what he was born to write but, it would seem, killing himself with unpublishable prose, not to mention drink.

It was Hermann Hagedorn, his future biographer, who got the poet to go to the MacDowell Colony in Peterborough, New Hampshire. The two had met the previous summer, and now, at the instigation of George Pierce Baker with whom Hagedorn was working, the younger man set out to conquer the Robinsonian prejudice against "artists' colonies." Subconsciously, if not consciously, Robinson must have known that he was in a bad way, that something had to be done, that either he found a way to regularize his life and a way back to poetry, or he would go down. And this time there would be no way back. He went to the MacDowell Colony in the summer of 1911 with a faked telegram in his pocket to show to Mrs. MacDowell, just in case things turned out as he feared they would at this "artists' colony." As he had run away from New York to Chocorua, so now he had an escape hatch ready should all the "artists" prove too much. He stayed, and stayed for good. From this time on he would divide his life between Peterborough and various friends' houses in Boston, New York, Gardiner. He was a sick man when he came to Peterborough, a man whose hold on life had become precarious. Liquor had finally become indispensable to him, and the work he was doing in prose had, it would seem, the air of unreality that an obvious escape sometimes has. He must have felt that as long as he worked, no matter how worthless the result (and he had to know the work was bad, at his age) he could claim the title of author and a right to drink long and hard. Peterborough cured him. He found friends, a few admirers, solitude, natural beauty, an atmosphere where work attracted and compelled. He gave up liquor. That summer reclaimed him in large measure, yet he still had the double problem of money and a way to do what he must: write poetry.

Winter found him once more in the grip of that lust for the stage that he seemed to have got over. He had to have a last fling at it, though, if only to prove finally to himself that he could not do it. And of course, he knew that when he should finally so fail, he would go back to writing poetry and "starving in a hole," as he put it. He was forty-three years old. Now as before what saved him was the devotion of friends. He lived intermittently with Louis Ledoux, or the Hagedorns, and returned to the lion-hunting Mrs. Davidge who had removed her establishment to Staten Island along with an artist gentleman friend whom she subsequently married, presumably. Very possibly it took the heat off the poet. During this time his prose fiction made the rounds of the publishers and duly returned. Late in that year 1912–13 he woke from the dream of dramatic success, as he had to sooner or later if he was not to perish there, and wrote Hays Gardiner that ". . . I perpetrate the damndest rubbish you ever heard of. . . . At last I can see the light again, and I am going to write another book of poems."

So much is speculation! Why did he give up so suddenly and so gladly, as it appears, his infatuation? At the risk of repetition, I suggest that he could exist for himself only in the act of writing or at any rate as one who wrote and would write as long as he could breathe. Hagedorn observes of his kind friends the Taylors (she was the former Mrs. Davidge) that "they did not take him seriously as a man, which cut him to his most sensitive nerve." Hagedorn, who knew Robinson well, may be assumed to speak from certain and probably first-hand information on a matter of this sort; what he implies in his remark has considerable importance. I believe that Robinson, single and single-minded as he was, yet invested great feeling in friends and his nieces and sister-in-law. He obviously put all there was left into poetry. When, therefore, he came to dry periods in his poetic life he had recourse to friends, liquor and other sorts of writing to get him through the desert. Sometimes friends failed, as the Taylors did, and no doubt he asked too much of them, as such persons as he are likely to do. They most quietly, and therefore most insistently, demand a kind of emotional attention and commitment that many people cannot give, for whatever reasons. Fortunately for Robinson, and largely because his nature once known responded so fully to those who cared to know, a very considerable number of people gave unstintingly of their time, affection, trust and money—and more than any of these, they believed in the poems. This last unlocked to any man or woman Robinson's affection and loyalty. Love me, love my poems—or poetry, anyhow. It seems to me that such people as the Taylors tried to dissociate the poet and the man, and that is precisely what EA would not have. Had he not fought for twenty-five years to bring together into a single sense or sensibility all the conflict of idealism, materialism, personal tragedy, cosmic optimism, burning ambition and intimate knowledge of failure? How on earth could anyone try to remove a man from his deepest experience? Poetry is not something you do, it is something you are. Perhaps there may be a few Brownings whose case so puzzled Henry James and Hardy, but Robinson had lived the life of his poetry to the full and had gone to the bottom to bring it back to light. Now, in this time of dryness, he needed to sink new wells. Another poet might have turned to translation or to autobiography, as so many have, but this particular poet wrote himself out of the desert with bad plays and fiction. The regimen worked, but the ultimate effects were, I think, unhappy in that they tended to confirm in him certain tendencies toward melodrama and an overqualified garrulity of style that we have already seen as a danger.

But he had reached a turning point by 1913. His reputation had grown in spite of resistance. There was a new climate in letters. The pioneer work of Pound, particularly as advocate of the new and the new poets, had begun to be felt. Harriet Monroe's *Poetry* may be said to have brought to the United States the message: "Tell them in America that poetry is an Art." Thus Pound, in his categorical imperative to Harriet Monroe. They needed telling and they would soon find proof. But meantime, for Robinson himself, the dam had begun to crumble. The *Atlantic* succumbed and bought poems, one suspects strongly because of an interview with Robinson in the Boston *Post* which in turn had been prompted by a statement in the Boston *Evening Transcript* by Alfred Noyes to the effect that Robinson was the best American poet writing. Impeccable auspices! The *Transcript*—and Mr. Noyes! Even the *Atlantic* must succumb, an *Atlantic* which in the previous twenty years had published exactly one of EA's poems, "Vickery's Mountain," and that in the "In Lighter Vein" section at the back, as they say, of the book. All the while, of course, giving vast space to those monumental fakes whose work so often gets in the way of their betters. But the dam now was indeed broken. The summers of 1913–16 at Peterborough saw the greatest period of production of his career, and the magazines, notably *Poetry,* enshrined some of the finest results of that fruitful time. The great power of the work shows plainly in the 1916 volume, *The Man Against the Sky.* Whatever one may decide with respect to the poem that gives the book its title, one still must say that at least eight of the poems in this volume rank with the poet's very best, which is to say, with the best then being written in English or American or any combination thereof. He had indeed got through the desert; those three years between his re-emergence from the dream of playwriting and the publication of *The Man Against the Sky* saw the re-establishment of the old rhythm: winter meant gestation and assimilation while he lived in New York or with friends here and there or both; spring, summer and fall meant Boston and Peterborough and writing into poems what the months before had slowly brought to the surface. This newest volume displays Robinson's talent handsomely and variously: the blank verse monologue, handled with great ease and economy ("Ben Jonson Entertains a Man from Stratford"); the tight, emphatic lyric ("Veteran Sirens"); the ruminating yet compact reflective lyric ("Eros Turannos" or "The Poor Relation"); the verse portrait ("Bewick Finzer"); the ironic compressed narrative ("Old Trails"). Each of these types has more than one exemplar in this volume, nor is there an ill-conceived, boring or lazy work to be found. Hereafter, matters will change, though for about ten more years Robinson still summons the power to write fine poems of short to medium length. Still, it can be said that this book is the last to show all major aspects of Robinson's major talent, without lapses and with a sense of total mastery. Some of his very finest lyrics are still to come, and two or three of the blank verse monologues, but apart from the achievement in the long narratives, for whatever that may be worth, no other single title will rank with this one.

VI

The Man Against the Sky

The poem of the name has had a contradictory reception. The poetry lovers and Robinsonophiles have taken it as a masterpiece, whereas critics and other odd sorts and conditions of reader almost to a man condemn it as overblown, reactionary and intellectually trivial. Yvor Winters puts the latter case well and with the usual conciseness we associate with his comments: "Philosophically, the poem is unimpressive; stylistically it is all quite as weak as the lines referred to above [lines 26–32]; and structurally, it seems to defeat its purpose—for while it purports to be an expression of faith, it is devoted in all save these same few lines to the expression of despair." What Winters says here has validity, but it tends to beg the question, as do most of the strictures on the poem. All start with the assumption that the poem is a philosophical statement which simply does not sort well with its form and which comes to no reasonable or logical conclusion. One hates to use the word existential, but we can grit our teeth and put it this way: Robinson, in this poem, sets up his favorite dualities of soul-mind, materialism-idealism, meaning-nothing. The poem contains echoes of such others of his works as the very early "The Torrent" and the nearly contemporaneous "Hillcrest." In spirit and impulse it goes back to the "Octaves" and looks forward to his last published poem, *King Jasper.* We see therefore that here is one of the central, the defining problems of this poem, one which defines an aspect of his gift and his work. All his life he had worried the ontological question and when he came at it most directly in the poems, readers today are least likely to respond. The

ways in which he frames the question of themselves put off
many readers, and the fact that he emerges with neither answers nor a conclusion that the question after all does not
exist makes the existentially inclined impatient and contemptuous. But the poem must be regarded as a personal and eloquent
assessment of man's possible fates in a certain moment in
history. As such, it takes its place with Stevens' "Sunday Morning"
as one of the great twentieth-century American assaults on the
unassailable—both poems do what no other poet has since even
attempted, though some are careful enough to assure us that
such attempts are by definition fruitless and hence unpoetic.
They did not seem so to Robinson nor to Stevens. And one
might add, the Eliot of "Little Gidding" has rather more in
common with them than the Eliot of "The Waste Land."

"The Man Against the Sky" is old-fashioned, awkward at
times, both metrically and syntactically. It is too long and
piles on the abstractions too heavily. Yet there are fine Wagnerian moments, great eloquence and a sense that here is a
poet who dares take the risk of bathos, stumbling sometimes,
yet somehow getting to places most have only heard of. I do
not for a moment contend that the poem is in itself the equal
of either "Sunday Morning" or "Little Gidding"; for one thing
it belongs to another tradition, for another it specifically rejects both the Anglo-Catholic religion of Eliot and the aesthetic
paganism of Stevens, coming down hard on the far more modern
(if that is any recommendation) principle of the certainty of
uncertainty. The provenience of the poem is Romantic, Ten-
nysonian, and transcendental. Where Stevens would find immortality in the things of this world, his "physical world," and
Eliot would find his "whispers of immortality" in a rose, a symbol of blood, purgation, fire and resurrection, Robinson characteristically sees man as caught in the middle, on an "isthmus
of a middle state / A being darkly wise and rudely great," as
Pope has it. His images here, as in many another Robinson
poem, have to do with middle height, dropping down to water,
a lurid sky. Where Eliot is liturgical, Robinson is biblical; where
Stevens invokes and evokes the sensuousness of earth, Robinson
calls on history, the flux of atoms, entropy. Interestingly, in
these three poems, the concluding image, in each case, the image

which dominates the whole, is of descent, yet in each case the differences count most heavily. Eliot gives us "the dove descending," the Holy Spirit; Stevens, the "casual" pigeons which in their descent into dark make "ambiguous undulations"; and Robinson his modern and hopeless Job who looks out on the shores and the "tideless floods of Nothingness / Where all who know may drown."

The chief point for all three poets lies in the realization that man must place himself in harmony with the universe or with God. Man tries to know, and knowing can lead to disaster, since what is only intellectual can only and finally deceive. Robinson's "all who know" are those who know with the intellect only, as Stevens' "ring of men" represents man in his passional, instinctual and wholly natural state without mere mind, and as Eliot's command to modern man is to "be still and know that I am God." To many contemporary readers, the message of Stevens has greatest appeal, inasmuch as he simply takes for granted the fact that "god is dead," and a good thing too; Eliot and his arcane Anglicanism strike many as obscurantist, irrelevant; and Robinson's old-fashioned struggle to reconcile materialism and idealism rather shocks with its persistent concern for an issue long since joined but simply ignored because it went *on* so; better forgotten about. I dwell on the differing approaches of these three great American representative men of poetry because coming into their power when and as they did shows much about their time. All three have certain common concerns, chief among which is a search for meaning otherwhere than in flux, but allied to this, a passionate desire to mean beyond the moment and beyond oneself. Each poet differs widely from the others in all imaginable ways; what they share apart from country of origin and poetic genius is Harvard, which can hardly be said to link men closely, as noted in the old story of that most democratic of Harvard crewmen and scion of the stock of Saltonstall who knew well every man in his boat—"except a couple of fellows up in the bow." Today we find uncomfortable, and indeed tactless, an appetite for eternal verities; we are more than likely to use the standard scientific-philosophic escape of claiming that they do not exist, that questions which arise from a consideration of them lack validity.

Stevens simply declares that not to live in a physical world, or conversely, to live in a world of concepts, is the great disaster. Poetry, the supreme fiction, makes a physical world for us. Eliot contends that we try to escape from time into the timeless and from the material into immateriality without reckoning what we are about; only through the actualities of this world can one come to the next. And Robinson tells us that man's whole nature speaks to him a "Word," gives him a "Vision," and these have so great a part in human nature that when we as it were deliberately suppress our power of apprehension of them we suffer despair, what the knowing would call anomie, "Nothingness." Indeed, this Latter Job would do right to "curse God and Die," except that since there is no longer any god, man cannot afford the luxury of the curse.

What we can find after confronting three assaults on the universe such as "Little Gidding," "Sunday Morning," and "The Man Against the Sky" are three characteristically modern and yet timeless responses to man's fate, existentially considered: Eliot's Christian quietism, Stevens' neo-pagan aestheticism, Robinson's transcendental idealism. No other poets of the century writing in English have even so much as attempted the questions these three both put and try to answer. One knows now why a critic tells us that nowadays we do not read poetry for wisdom. "The Man against The Sky" not only deals in questions and answers, or approaches to answers, but does so in the form of an ode of the Horatian sort, dithyrambic perhaps or as much so as Robinson could manage, and above all rhetorical, in the better and worse senses of that term. The rhetoric is romantic and in the by this time almost anonymous vein of "classical" Romanticism; the nominal subject is "the nature and destiny of man"; and the tone is one of loftiness occasionally tempered with cosmic irony. We must, I believe, count the poem a failure, certainly in comparison with the other two discussed here. Yet it has importance in the development of Robinson's later career, as well as in itself. On it the career pivots, as it were, and the poetry that comes after will re-echo much that is sounded here. Intrinsically, though, the poem has great value and the rhetoric can be said to work and work well in the opening and closing lines, not to mention in those parts of the

poem which, biblical in provenience, have a fine Old Testa-
mentary swing to them. An old-fashioned poem.

"Gad, how I love reasoning in verse," says the protagonist
of *The Rehearsal*. If we do not quite catch Robinson saying as
much here or in many of the narratives of the following years,
we may still feel that we often catch him enjoying the ruminating, ramifying pattern of his ratiocinative versifying. "The Man
Against the Sky" has more power than most of the later long
poems simply because it has a certain epigrammatic lyricism
and keeps to strict rhyme and meter. His poetry nearly always
benefits from such order, and the ideas and reasoning of the
poem at least seem more logical as a result. But whatever we
may finally call the mental processes at work in the poem, we
at last come face to face with that vexed matter of Robinson's
philosophy.

I have said that I believe he has no philosophy as such, a
statement I base partly on a reading of the poetry, partly on
what he himself said, partly on what I think I know of poetry
and poets in general. Which is not to say that poets do not or
cannot think, though it is to say that they think effectively as
poets when they think according to the inner dynamics of the
poem. For example, the famous dictum of Sainte-Beuve that
Yeats appropriated—"the will doing the work of the imagination"—applies in many instances. The early "Octaves" strike
me as feeble poetically because one of the results of inadequate
thought in art is bad art, which in a work of literature means,
among other things, intellectual non-sense. Who would take this
to mean that Robinson did not "mean" these poems? No one,
I hope: he wrote them out of a real need and with the purpose
of confirming himself in an attitude or conviction which ran
counter to his deepest feelings. Again and again these poems
seem to confront a real problem, then dissipate themselves in
cloudy rhetoric. Once in a while, as in "Octave XI" there will
come a fine phrase, indeed a group of lines, with a nice ironic
flourish:

> . . . and thus we die
> Still searching, like poor old astronomers
> Who totter off to bed and go to sleep
> To dream of untriangulated stars.

Some of them have to do with the poet and his art; some, in fact nearly all, deal with the question of "knowledge" as opposed to "thought." But the poems get nowhere. They do not provoke intellection nor do they open out speculatively; the writing is on a level of abstraction so high that it reminds more of a certain sort of hymnody than of poetry, as the diction and rhetoric savor of transcendental Romanticism at their most inflated: "the still crash of salvatory steel," "thought's impenetrable mail," and so on—really bad writing but a young man's bad writing, derivative and deliberately pretentious, very nearly devoid of meaning beyond that of the most banal. But again I emphasize that Robinson was honest and meant honestly. The Emersonian Christian Science of these poems shows, if nothing else, the poverty of the purely intellectual material he had to work with, as the language and tone-deaf versification show how run-out was the very tradition he here attempted to revivify.

The failures in "Octaves" recur, in some measure, in "The Man Against the Sky" but with the great difference I have already noted of technique as well as another difference, that here Robinson has a subject in hand, one that goes deep, if not quite deep enough to find one of the great poems, at least far deeper than "Octaves" ever went. The poem is about "knowing" and what has ceased to be called "thought" and is now "seeing." The first four strophes make clear, eloquent statements, by any standard but the immediately contemporary, both witty and lyrical. The rhythms and rhymes are firm, compact, epigrammatic when they depart from the flow of the more romantic lines. Robinson sets up the situation, the problem, the dilemma (that of man in a world that is inscrutable and perhaps hostile). The rest of the poem will deal, logically enough, with all the "varieties of religious experience" or refusal thereof which the poet finds germane to his subject. Here, then, is a truly dramatic and lyrical attack on a metaphysical—a cosmic—question. Here if anywhere, we might suppose, we shall find the key to all mystery, the "figure in the carpet," the philosophy that lurks behind the enigmatic guise.

What in fact do we find? Well, we can give a few of Robinson's sketches of attitudes portentous Latinate labels, like rare shrubs which turn out to be privet or box: we can call specimen one the Solipsist; two, the Stoic; three, the Materialist, and so on through the list that Robinson consulted to provide himself with a full crop of more or less popular attitudes towards the ontological question. But the fact remains that there is not an idea or a philosophical process, conclusion or suggestion in the poem. The mise en scène, after all, combines Wagner's *Götterdämmerung* and the fall landscape of New England, the country of "Luke Havergal" and "The Dark Hills," both variants of the theme here explored at large. True enough, Robinson provides here more than a little abstraction, a trace or so of that periphrastic obscurity that could obsess and delude him; yet finally we have to confess that what gives the poem vitality and relevance lies in the sense it gives of a lived, and earned, a felt attitude. Robinson has been there; he knows, and he has survived and come back to tell us. How different from "Octaves" with the obvious rhetorical effort to pump up style and feeling, to give an effect of profundity. Robinson had, by the time of "The Man Against the Sky," been through enough to know that if a philosophy meant anything to a poet, it could mean it only in a sense so loose as to disqualify as meaning. The poem deals with "Hell, Heaven and Oblivion"—that and no more. Enough, isn't it? Both Stevens and Eliot found it so. But as Stevens said "The greatest poverty is not to live / In a physical world." Robinson was not the first poet, nor the last, to find that what has roots in the actual bears the finest poetic fruit. In his years at Harvard, the courses in philosophy he attempted were his despair, as the study of the law was for Henry James. Not philosophy but the human comedy fascinated both writers; but while James saw men and woman as intricate parts of elaborate patterns of divergent cultures, Robinson saw men as in part toys of Hardyesque "purblind doomsters" and slaves of an almost heroic self-delusion, like the superannuated whores of his "Veteran Sirens," who are so "alert for learning how / To fence with reason for another year." Philosophy, as a formal or informal scheme, solves no one's personal and cosmic problems in these poems. What study, what labor, what speculation will ever satisfy a man as to what "inexorable cause / Makes Time so vicious in his reaping"? If we can find anything at all of the craving for "ideas" in Robinson, we must I suppose come to the point of what he chooses to lump under the generic term or symbol of "light." We shall deal with that problem when we come to the Arthurian poems and *Lancelot.* To conclude the discussion of "The Man Against the Sky" and the philosophical problem, I think it right for us to see our poet as poet and as perplexed man, suffering man. When the suffering and perplexity find distance, irony, perspective, wit, we can see one of the fine Robinsons at work; when they find immediacy in a person in a situation, compressed and essential, we can see perhaps the finest Robinson. He had what Shaw called "the metaphysical appetite," and he wanted to know, finally, to resolve doubt once and for all, not to suffer forever from the disease of modern life that Arnold describes in "The Scholar Gypsy," showing modern men as "light half-believers of our casual creeds." Stevens could go on to do precisely what Arnold recommended and make a religion of poetry; Eliot could revert to Anglicanism; but Robinson, unchurched forever by his legacy of attenuated Calvinism and Emersonianism, vacillated between abstract and concrete, between seeing and believing, between dark and light, "where all who know may drown."

But the volume which bears the title of that poem contains another which does all the things the great ode does not—simply, quietly, without recourse to strictly "literary" expedients. That poem is "Hillcrest," dedicated to Mrs. MacDowell and written at the Colony. The theme of between worlds comes before us at once, in the first two stanzas, here on this "island in a sea of trees" and "between the sunlight and the shade." A calm, true and lived poem, autumnal as to tone, feeling, imagery and setting. That the poem comes from Robinson's convictions about his own life and career seems evident from the rather unusual particularity of these elements. He dedicated the poem to Mrs. MacDowell, perhaps as much in apology for his original misgivings about the Colony as in tribute; he knew she would appreciate the irony. The process begun during the months spent with Bartlett in Chocorua reached a fulfillment in Peterborough, in Robinson's cabin where he could sit and look at Mount Monadnock, achieving a kind of ease and peace with nature that he had never known and which indeed we know he had for whatever reason avoided. Perhaps the contemplation of natural beauty, too frequently a source of automatic ecstasies in the poetry of the time, repelled him; we know, at any rate, that he rather particularly disavowed, at the beginning of his career, any link with Romantic and regional nature worship. He wrote to Arthur Gledhill just before his first book came out that "there is very little tinkling water, and there is not a red-bellied robin in the whole collection. When it comes to 'nightingales and roses' I am not 'in it.' . . ." And we also recall that he feared the encounter with nature that his stay in the White Mountains with Bartlett made inevitable. He had said that "this place is a heavy dose [of nature] for a neophyte but I see that I am going to like it. My only fear is that I may like it too well . . ." In the four or five years between the stay with Bartlett and the writing of "Hillcrest," something happened and that something derived at least in part from his giving in, as it were, to what we will have to call, in Wordsworth's phrase, "the influence of natural objects." Peterborough, the MacDowell Colony and Mount Monadnock provided the scene, the ambience, the objects themselves; the rest was the work of healing which those things set in motion.

Robinson had been too near to despair too long, near the breaking point too long. Now at last a rumor of fame began to grow about him, a sense that he existed as a poet and a man took hold, his place in a natural world began to seem possible, real. These years brought him peace and some of his finest poems. In "Hillcrest" we find his own testimony as to the hell he had lived through and the beneficent powers which restored him and made him see that should he be required to live there again, he could bear it. It does not do, of course, to claim that "nature" had sole charge and must take all the credit. People helped him, as they always had. Time itself may have had a hand in the work, though as a rule time simply deprives a man of the capacity to care very much. One gets older. Still I think we can say that if the disasters attendant upon the career of *Captain Craig* stunted Robinson's growth, ended his youth prematurely, the autumnal but by no means melancholy years between 1910 and 1916 brought him to the peak of his poetic powers.

"Hillcrest" is an example of a poet thinking and feeling his way perfectly through his poem. The idiom has the simple, natural strain that marks the best work, yet all is tight, economical and beautifully intricate in so subtle a way that the reader does not have to keep telling himself what fine effects the poet is getting.

> No sound of any storm that shakes
> Old island walls with older seas
> Comes here where now September makes
> An island in a sea of trees.

The opening lines not only establish the tone—muted, contemplative, grave—but sound certain words, like notes, which belong to tone, of course, but which also gather an increasing increment of meaning as they recur throughout the poem. Sound, storm, seas, islands, September, trees; all these singly and together assume a complex of meaning which one hesitates to ascribe to a symbolic source. The key to the matter is not so much symbolism as incremental repetition and the layers of significance acquired. And as so often is the case, the verb "see," with all that for readers of Robinson "seeing" implies of true understanding and revelation, controls imagery, the whole intellectual movement of the poem. In the second stanza, we find the phrase "between the sunlight and the shade," and we might take it as characterizing the tone, the attitude, the very world that the poem exploits and explores. In this end-of-summer time, a man looks about him and begins to see something not only of the real world but of himself and his place in that world. For the first time. The poem is about growing up, about being a man, about facing one's illusions at last, and going on without them.

One of the most remarkable things about this poem is its diction. For the most part abstract, it yet remains simple, transparent, clear. Every so often a sudden specific natural image strikes with the greater impact because of its unexpectedness and its power of summation. There are three such images or clusters of images and each links the physical and the mental or emotional very particularly. In stanza six the image of the oaks returning to acorns; in stanza eleven, that of the illusioned child; in the final stanza, that of the web of error and its sound like the falling of leaves: these three clusters quietly perform poetic tasks of expression, summary and signification which testify not only to the poem's complexity but also to its economy. Much of what Robinson has to say here some readers are bound to dislike; it is not fashionable to contemplate one's "ruins and regrets" nor to see childhood as something other than perfection, nor will many readers ever attune themselves to such statements as the poem explicitly makes as well as implicitly signifies. Stoicism has a poor reputation, but it is a Roman virtue and Robinson is a Roman among barbarians. A line-by-line analysis of this work might exhaust our patience but not the poem; yet I myself feel that it is so clear, simple and profound that no exegesis can help much beyond pointing at a few characteristics and letting the reader approach the poem with as little irrelevancy of preconception as possible. It is a poem about life and death and change and growth and their interaction, and it is a masterpiece.

It is a counter-Romantic masterpiece, interestingly. Always in Robinson we find that duality, that casting back and forth between poles. Just when he has gone-all-over-Emerson on us, he brings us up hard with a tough, almost brutal, account of the hard facts of a particular case. In the poem under consideration the toughness is latent, but we sense under the rueful delicacy of speech a stoic and humane resilience, endurance. It is, above all, speech, a man speaking to men, with subtle humor and a disenchanted, ironic view of the self. One has to be alert to such quiet effects, particularly in times when Wordsworth's "gross stimulants" are the order of the day. Robinson does not get our attention by cracking us in the face nor by insult—perfectly valid ways of seizing the attention. But Robinson wants to tease and provoke us to consideration. "Hillcrest" perfectly fulfills its intent and that intent is large, complex, profound. Pairing it with "The Man Against the Sky" both emphasizes the fineness of the former while it exposes the element of bombast in the latter. In his attempt to write a formal set piece that should monumentally stand for the Romantic ontological dilemma, Robinson found himself trying by means of a rhetoric to thrash his way out of banalities into original thought. As we have seen, the attempt is not without tactical successes, though a strategic defeat ensues; the language betrays poet and poem at certain crucial points, and what tries to pass for objective intellectual penetration of a human dilemma looks more like words overlaying something rather simple. We cannot doubt Robinson's honesty because the question he torments has reality and much of what he says comes through as real and moving. But the fault lies in a rhetoric which betrays him into bombast, and the rhetoric, in turn, grew from a mistaken approach to theme and subject. "Hillcrest" makes no mistakes, is personal without subjectivity, candid without the confessional, lyrical without self-pity.

It may well be that Robinson, during these fruitful years, spent a great deal of time in a kind of retrospection, thinking and remembering back into youth and childhood. He was in his forties and at such a time a man is likely to start assessing himself, seeing how far short of his aims he has fallen, how lucky he has been to have made it thus far, how mysterious the ways that brought him here. He will look to the future again when he is fifty, as he did when he was in his thirties, but now he remembers, regrets, marvels. A number of the poems in this volume seem to suggest that the years between 1910 and 1916 gave him both peace and a new self-confidence. "Ben Jonson Entertains a Man from Stratford" with its clear portrait of the artist, "Veteran Sirens" with its incisive yet tender view of the aging whores he knew in Boston and New York, "The Poor Relation" with its moving and sympathetic portrayal of loneliness, "The Gift of God" with its ironic view of a mother's love for her son: all these come straight out of Robinson's own inner and outer experience; they are his "life studies" but made, like "Hillcrest," exemplary through fiction rather than expressive through emotionalism. We do not need to know that Robinson's mother preferred his brothers to him in order to understand "The Gift of God"; we are required only to read the words on the page. It was a method he recommended to a lady (one is sure it was no woman but a lady) who asked him what to do, she found his poetry so difficult, and he replied that she should try reading it, "one word after another." True, anyone can misunderstand anything, and when Robinson wrote in rueful indignation that one reviewer had said that the poem was "a touching tribute to Our Savior," he touched on one sort of obtuseness that every poet can expect to encounter. Many readers have remarked on what they take to be at the very least an analogy to Mary and Jesus, with all the variations on that analogical theme one might expect and a number one would not. Of course, such an analogy is preposterous; Robinson may in the poem have intended an ironic echo or so—no more. Robinson tends to write stories, fictions; he writes in "The Gift of God" about a mother who, like many mothers, adores and idealizes a son who, like many sons, is composed of the base metal most of us are composed of, a metal the mother, by an alchemy of her own, can "transmute," and have him "shining where she will." The fact that her son's great career "as upward through her dream he fares" is delusionary, in fact a "dream," does not detract from the power of her love; on the contrary, it reinforces it, whether for good or ill Robinson does not say, but irony spins the plot and we can guess. Robinson never married but he knew a thing or two about love, and one of them was that some variants of love, love cannot forgive. "The laugh that love could not forgive" we remember from "For a Dead Lady." Mary Palmer Robinson, like many another refined, lovely, otherworldly woman before and since, was a powerful creature and made her mark on her husband and her sons. In "The Gift of God" one of those sons looks closely and sees a few things we might have expected him to have missed or hidden.

Similarly, we do not need to know—though how good to know it—that Robinson frequented whorehouses in Boston and was a rather good friend of at least one of the working girls. Our only testimony as to the matter speaks exclusively of his college years and nothing of the years that followed. No other sexual experience as such has its witnesses of partners or ascribers or fictionists. I am not myself aware of any attempt to establish Robinson as a homosexual though I feel sure that it has been and will be made. The question of what used to be known as love (as opposed to sex?) life seems to confine itself to mysterious hints as to the identity of Chard Powers Smith's "girl of the woodland walks" and the assumption that his only love was Emma, Herman's wife and widow. Any number can play, of course. But the poem "Veteran Sirens" shows pretty conclusively that the poet knew something about prostitution as a way of life and as a form of escape into unreality as efficacious as the kind he described in "Hillcrest" and "The Gift of God." He seems to say in many of these poems that to face facts and then go on, cheerfully and without illusions, requires extraordinary courage, endurance, self-knowledge. Or at any rate, self-control. Remarkable to reflect that some critics expressed shock and dismay when Yvor Winters wrote that the poem dealt with "old prostitutes," but such reactions are of a piece with the assumption that Mary and Jesus have to do with "The Gift of God." Which is finally to say that it is no wonder that Robinson—and he was speaking for many another poet as well as himself—burst out occasionally: "Why don't they *read* me?" Yet such "doctrinal adhesions" crop up in anyone's mind and in any context; misreading is common. We as readers have only one duty, which is to know that we too can and do misread and to accept correction when it occurs.

"The Poor Relation" may not reach a considerable audience today, not so much because it can be misread as because the very subject does not speak to the modern American, who has no relations anyhow and who does not admit to poverty, death or total defeat of the spirit. Here is a poem which deals with one of the phenomena our society hides or specifically rejects as non-existent. There are no such creatures as this desolate, broken woman, alone and waiting for death in her city apartment. Interestingly, Robinson does not speak of the classical old small-town New England spinster, the sort familiar to those who grew up in a world not as unlike Robinson's own as ours is unlike our children's. This poor relation, paid to go away and hide herself as it seems, exchanging (she has no alternative) any possible independence for "security," which is to say money, exists by herself, in the past and her dead youth, and with neither illusion nor hope to inspirit. She merits the "poor" as epithet because, ironically, she lacks everything that makes life tolerable—*except* money. She is well enough kept—"safe in a comfortable cage"—but has very nearly dropped out of humanity; those rare few who come to visit do not stay long: "Pity having played soon tires," as the poem has it; nor does she by this time expect anything. Part of the richness and allusiveness of the poem comes from the hints Robinson gives of her past and how she affected others. In a masterly fashion he gives us the sense of a rather beautiful young girl and woman who, through misfortune, envy of others, the inability to be tough and fight back, and perhaps a sickness which may be physical but might well have psychological aspects, has given up a struggle which she now fully accepts as lost—yet accepts somehow with a humility and selflessness that can only be beautiful. The last two stanzas of this poem have a nearly intolerable intensity of pathos; aesthetically and humanly, the poem is extraordinarily moving, and perhaps the more so for its very ordinariness of subject and theme. Here are no vastations, epiphanies, cosmic speculations, psychodramatics; here are the facts of desolation, deprivation, loneliness. Curiously, or perhaps not so curiously, the poem which this most nearly resembles would seem to be "For a Dead Lady." Stanza and metrical pattern are almost identical, and indeed both are of a sort favored by Robinson and the vehicle of some of his finest lyrics, if lyrics they are. The alternate masculine and feminine rhymes give emphasis and a kind of bite; we note particularly in the last two stanzas how the sound of the city—New York, one feels sure—surrounds the woman and envelops her with its torturing hum "like a giant harp," and the sounds of the city mingle with those of time itself, the ticking of clocks, the beating of the blood, until they seem a kind of water-torture, "like slow drops descending." "For a Dead Lady," this poem, "Eros Turannos": the three form a triad and represent certain forms of loss, despair and defeat which Robinson will not try to explain nor excuse but with which he simply confronts the reader. "For a Dead Lady" and "Eros Turannos" have more power of shock, of narrative and of assault, but "The Poor Relation" is the most simply moving. The three together would make any poet's reputation, and most get by on far less!

Here again, as is the case with just about all the poems of *The Man Against the Sky*, we find our poet thinking, feeling and composing simultaneously—acts of the total imagination. One might spend pages—and I have done so elsewhere—examining certain of the techniques and images in "Eros Turannos," for example, or "The Gift of God." Robinson could write verse as cunningly "metaphysical" as that of his successors, but without the fanfare and the explication de texte that the poet-critics provided for themselves and one another. He understood his craft, having learned it over many years from the best teachers of as they say creative writing, whatever that may exactly be, and those teachers are of course the great and good poems. There aren't any others—just professors. But Robinson did not give readings nor did he write about his poetry or anyone else's. With the exception of a very brief essay in the old *Colophon* published in 1930, he wrote nothing for publication about his work or what I believe is termed the "creative process," which I would think an obstetrician would know more about, or maybe a mother. But he had his notions and his prejudices, as which poet hasn't, and he had moreover a little less regard for fashion or current opinion than do most poets, which is only of course to say that most poetry in any age is bad and that the good poetry is likely to get written by poets who can manage to avoid the rush.

This is what Robinson had to say about two poets: "Do you know I have a theory that Browning's life-long happiness with his wife is all humbug? The man's life was in his art . . ." This in a letter to Smith. And to Hays Gardiner he wrote, "Donne doesn't seem to me to interpret much more than a sort of half-mystical sexual uneasiness and a rather uninteresting religious enthusiasm which seems to have been quite the thing in those days for a fellow who had raised the devil for thirty-five or forty years and so worked up an appetite for symbols." Small wonder the New Critics and their epigoni ignored or dismissed him, Donne being their patron saint. But styles and times and civilizations change. With luck, much that is good from them survives. "Love builds of what Time takes away, / Till Death itself is less than Change." So "Hillcrest" has it. It is a good Robinsonian last word.

VII

A Digression on Obscurity

Strange that a man who rejects the notion that he cannot understand ideas rejoices in his powerlessness to understand the simplest poem. Poetry is obscure. The psychology of obscurity as a perceived enigma would make a fascinating study, but here and now we need to examine why many readers and critics in Robinson's time found his work obscure. And first of all, let us admit that it often is, if by "obscure" we mean that many of his poems are so boring and syntactically involuted that we lack the patience to decode them. Such a failure defines the first sort of obscurity we shall isolate: bad writing—lazy, self-indulgent writing—makes "cursed hard reading." Contrary to what the experts think, ease and grace of style do not make a superficial writer, nor does a crabbed text make a masterpiece. Poets have weaknesses, and all poets with a marked manner tend at times to imitate themselves, to imitate poems, and that invariably results in bad work. Moreover, in a bad time, when a poet is too isolated, neglected and ignored, the tendency grows. Such is the case with Robinson.

Another kind of obscurity, often confused with the first, has to do with really original, difficult, complex ideas, conceptions, attitudes, of necessity expressed in unusual, perhaps repellent, language, rhythms, tropes. Poetry of this kind seems to emerge at transitional times; we might take Eliot's "The Waste Land" as an example. When the novelty and seeming chaos have been assimilated (a mere function of time) we often realize that the "obscurity" we encountered was really the shock of the unexpected. Robinson provided shocks of the kind, frequently by using "unpoetic" subjects and language in verse forms commonly associated with "poetic" matter, as for example in "Reuben Bright." But the real motive behind most allegations of obscurity comes from the reader's or critic's dislike of what the poet is saying. Wordsworth's detractors called him obscure; they meant that they disagreed with him. Most of Robinson's early critics called him obscure when what they meant was that he looked at certain things as they were and reported on that condition; he did not tell lies about how they looked. A younger but still contemporary poet, Hart Crane, was to call on his mythical and quasi-celestial Pocohontas to "lie to us! Dance us back our tribal morn!" He and Robinson are both obscure at times, and different as they are, both seem difficult for the same reason: they engage in a kind of automatic writing, self-imitative, logorrehic, either fatuous or plain boring. Neither poet can be called an original thinker, if by "thinker" we mean someone who deals primarily with conceptual thought and schematized systems of thought. Their originality consisted in their individual ways of looking at the world around them and reporting on how it looked and what it felt like to react to it in such ways. When the reactions to what they say seemed at odds with received critical views, critics then called them obscure.

There is another form of obscurity which really comes under the first mentioned: Crane dealt largely in this form as do certain poets of today. One might call it the mystagogic mode. Depending upon one's own choice of guru, one either likes or dislikes what a guru says. The mode itself requires only a basic sympathy with and infinite appetite for what we might call transcendence. Robinson as we have seen had a considerable appetite for these matters, but his vocabulary for them is founded upon a nineteenth-century rhetoric and a Protestant—perhaps really Unitarian—sense of the spiritual, the intense inane. Crane had an equally American Protestant spiritual appetite, but he lacked Robinson's biblical heritage and he had acquired a post-Symbolist, neo-Elizabethan rhetoric, occasionally infected by the Whitmanic. The modern mystagogues offer a compost of Orientalism, William Carlos Williams, and Poundian allusiveness. Now in all these cases, if you like that sort of thing, that is the sort of thing you will like. Browning is really the father of obscurity of this kind, and cultism necessarily follows. Some kinds of obscurity make of critics and readers a hermetic company of apostles, a chosen people. To read fanatics of the kind is to realize that obscurity for them has an absolute value wholly apart from meaning or a lack of it; indeed, obscurantism is the goal, the perfect concealment of sense. Pope wrote the *Dunciad* to show the humor and the horror of the condition.

And finally, obscurity can take on innocence, pretend to utter naïvety, hide in subtleties unremarked because so seemingly like banalities. Some of the best of Frost shows the kind, and of Robinson, too, yet in essence what we notice here is that the depth of any poem derives from this kind of "obscurity," in some measure. Some things some folk aren't fit to know and the things must be hid from them, so that only those found worthy can penetrate. Driven too far, such a strategy leads to some of the forms of difficulty or obscurity I have mentioned; handled with tact, it can account for some of the great poetic triumphs over chaotic states of feeling and perception.

Robinson often hides himself: Just as often he hides elements of the poem's "plot"; and he will sometimes hide the main character's motives and aims. Yet they lie there ready for the right kind of seeker. "Eros Turannos" we might call the locus classicus for his greatest triumphs in this strategy. Equally, he can fail and resort to mere trickery, using much the same strategic approach, as he does, I think, in "The Whip." The greatest failures, however, in his poetry and that of many another poet, occur when he hides himself from himself, not from others. That strategic failure, pursued to the end, seems to me to account for his long-windedness, prolixity and boring obfuscation. Unlike an underground movie, which requires no act or acts of attention, boring poetry requires as rigorous a minding as the most interesting, because it is not the poet's purpose to play the bore, as it is the avowed one of certain moviemakers, and we have to use our heads to find out if the poem is really a bore or if in fact it is a delayed-action bomb. To return to an early statement: bad poetry can look a great deal like good, and vice versa. One sometimes has to work to find the difference.

With Robinson's poetry the matter takes on an additional

complexity because, as we have seen, Robinson's poetry is in a low key, mutes its effects, and frequently looks boring when it in fact is not. The element of elliptical narrative in many cases puts off some readers; they find the surface of this poetry, plain and undecorated as it is, apparently sterile or perhaps simply repellent. By the same token, such readers dislike much of Wordsworth, "The Ruined Cottage," for example, and most of *The Prelude.* Much of the poetry of this sort that is muted, ruminative and in a middle style requires a kind of attention that some people fail to give because the return seems to them insufficient. They want more for their effort. We can see—have seen—cases in which Robinson bores us, but we need only call it that, not say he is obscure. Similarly, those who do not really penetrate the surface of much of the poetry have no right to call the work profound when it is merely wordy or derivative or both. "Octaves" for example are not obscure: they are bad because they imitate certain kinds of Romantic-Transcendental patterns of poetic jargon. It is no use asking what "thought's impenetrable mail" means, or what it is that "equitably un-creates itself." The matter has nothing to do with sense but everything to do with rhetoric. Obscurity of this kind is to the good poet what vulgarity and sentimentality are to the bad poet. In both cases the poet is trying to write so that he can write, get something going, only to find eventually that what he mistook for a poetic idea was reflection, echo. What is most truly obscure in a poem is the poet's attempt to hide his lack of meaning, the lack of a poetic idea. He has stopped thinking like a poet and thinks like a salesman, or like a man who writes not a poem but some poetry. Poets who write a lot and publish just about all of it must fall into that sin; no poet can write well always, and a number have more power of self-criticism, in the long run, and destroy the worst work before it sees print. Robinson wrote a great deal and must have suppressed very little. His isolation and unsuccess no doubt encouraged him to invest more feeling, and less judgment, in his poems than another poet might, with the result that he tended to feel that anything he wrote had value and validity because he wrote it, because it kept him going. When he runs on as he does in the long poems he did not seem ever to step back, or aside, to look at what he had done. He lived in the poetry as it came to him. We need not worry about it. A little practice quickly prepares us to find what is worth pursuing: if we are not caught up within ten lines, forget it and try elsewhere. When Robinson writes really well in a short poem, he will make us his in the first stanza, often the first line. Then if we do not "understand" when we come to the end, we will know why: the poem is, and is about, a mystery, as are most good poems.

VIII

The Downward Years,
1916–1927

The years of the Great War and those up to the year of
Tristram saw a change in Robinson's way of life in one sense:
the rhythm already established deepened, became settled, very
nearly final. The true center was still New York and that period
of hibernation and gestation; the epicenter, Peterborough and
four months of writing out what the winter had conceived.
After the Colony, Boston and perhaps some more writing, then
visits longer or shorter with friends like the Ledoux, and back
again to New York where he lived in a single room in a rooming house or a hotel, though later he moved to the James Earle
Frasers' house (on East 42nd Street) and spent most of his
winters thereafter with them. In a sense these were comfortable
years, perhaps a purist might say too comfortable, since most of
us feel that a poet is better for some kind of misery. But EA
had had his share, and so a number of his friends apparently
thought as early as 1919 when, at the instigation of a Peterborough resident—Lewis Isaacs, a composer and a successful
lawyer with considerable financial acumen, they decided to try
to make their friend the poet as free of monetary difficulties as
they could. A legacy which Hays Gardiner had left him was
gone; even in those days two thousand dollars could not keep
the most frugal forever. These friends found other friends willing
to contribute, and in December 1916 Robinson learned from the
New York Trust Company that from that time on for five years
he would be paid one hundred dollars a month, the source
remaining anonymous. Robinson seems to have been taken by

surprise, but not aback. If he did not exactly take the money as his due, he did not indulge in fulsome thanks. He may in fact have thought that perhaps he deserved it! However the rights of the case may go, the time seems to have been one of relative ease for him, physically at any rate.

Here again, as so often, we wonder about his inner life and what events, proven or speculative, of his self-effacing and sometimes mysterious career, affected, and how, the depths where the poems came from. Chard Powers Smith sees in the time a resurgence of the old love for Emma. There seems to be little doubt—as why should there be?—that he saw her occasionally over the years, though the ties with Tilbury Town and the House on Lincoln Avenue had gone rather slack. He still sent money to help his nieces and their mother, but just how close he felt to them, after all he had been through and with the increased and increasing wideness of his circle of friends, admirers and general acquaintance, is hard to say. We know from one or two comments in letters that he tried to get away from the past— his past—not exactly to forget or expunge memories, but to guard against them, not to "live" in the past, as he put it. And of course he always kept that inner life of his—and a good deal of the outer—in compartments. One set of friends knew nothing of another, and Ledoux claimed that it was not till after Robinson's death that he found out that the nieces who so adored their Uncle Win existed. Did he know of their mother's existence? No one, with the exception of Chard Powers Smith in his book, has suggested that a love for Emma was even a reality, let alone a long-lasting and determining reality. Smith claims that, in answer to a direct question, EA told him that he had portrayed his "great love" in the Guenevere of his *Lancelot*. Whether one should pursue the hint all the way, through betrayal and adultery and so on, remains moot. But the point seems to be that Robinson rather liked a little mystery in his life as he did in his poetry and in his reading; he was a mystery-story addict in his later years.

All his friends must have speculated about him and in particular about his putative celibacy, chastity, virginity, as you like it. Amusingly enough, several theories arose as to why and where he went on so many weekends away from Manhattan, and naturally no end of sexual suggestion ran rampant until it came out that most of the time he went to Brooklyn to see an old Gardiner friend, Seth Ellis Pope. But there did remain other unexplained removals!

Why is it poets seem to be catnip to women of a certain sort? The reputation for mystery, in Robinson's case, and for misogyny would clearly challenge any woman of normal hormones and unusual enterprise. All sorts and conditions of women tried it on, as the English say, but who made the scene? As far as we now know, nobody talked. Isadora Duncan's famous attempt is only the most flamboyantly unsuccessful of a number of others. Robinson liked women despite his shyness; some of his lifelong friends were women: Mrs. Richards, Edith Brower, Josephine (Peabody) Marks, and he got on well with the wives of his friends, by no means characteristic of single men, let alone artists. And indeed he seemed to relax in female company, not that it made him talk any more; only liquor and a great deal of it could work that miracle. It would seem to me that the women whom Robinson liked were of two sorts: older, rather powerful but not sexual opponents of any kind, and on the other hand those who were apparently vital, strongly sexed, often artistic or truly sympathetic to art (and artists!) and who could either leave him understandingly to his silences, or could tease him gracefully into response. In the period of Robinson's life under discussion, there seems to be a new ease which may well have derived from his growing awareness that as a poet, and hence as a man, he existed in the eyes of the world, and in his own. For all the years between the total failure of *Captain Craig* and the rumors of immortality that *The Man Against the Sky* seemed to circulate, he had lived in a kind of limbo; for a significant part of that time had failed to write at all, and for an equally significant period had written in the vain hope of making money and gaining fame. He had won neither, and instead had gone back to writing poetry, with a sense of relief, and in the perennial knowledge, so often expressed, that he could do nothing else. In one sense, he had touched bottom and had been irremediably hurt; in another sense, equally important, he had come to the final recognition that he had to fight the battle out on his chosen ground. It would appear that he had to come close to some kind of self-annihilation, by violence or alcohol, before he could let the principle of vitality in him, poetry, win out and take charge, but he came back very nearly from the dead, if that does not seem overdramatic. If it does, I would ask the reader to rehearse the facts of his life, the condition of the time, and his own imaginative response to these, particularly in the recurrence of the theme of rebirth.

By 1916 he was at work again, this time on a long project that he had been mulling over, consciously, since the year before. It would emerge as *Merlin* (1917), first of the three poems on Arthurian legend which culminated in *Tristram* and made his fortune, so to speak. One hesitates to call this group of three a trilogy, if only because *Tristram* comes ten years after *Merlin* and seven after *Lancelot;* the latter two seem much more of a piece than do all three and when everything is said and done, *Tristram* would seem to have the least power of survival; as he himself said, it was a conscious appeal to a wide public and can be called, I think, despite some genuine touches, the only meretricious performance of his career. But more of that later. What any reader of Robinson has to do is to take account of these first two Arthurian poems and consider them as poems in their own right and as indices of the direction or directions Robinson's career and maturing gift would take.

The Great War cannot here be ignored. From the start, Robinson had felt not that America should necessarily involve itself, but simply that it would be trapped in it. "We're all going to be caught in this," he said to Parker Fillmore when the Germans were driving towards Paris in their mismanaged compromise of the Schlieffen plan. Like his friend and fellow poet Moody, he had something less than total confidence in the American capacity for righteous war, benevolent imperialism, and enlightened capitalism. Both men saw war, and Robinson saw World War I in particular, as an imperialistic, capitalist adventure waged either blindly or for the purpose of protecting investments. For Robinson, however, the heart of the matter was his country's indifference to any but material values. He had already given some evidence of a discontent with democracy or aspects thereof, the most notable of these being his belief that American materialism made the citizen incapable of admiring and identifying true excellence and nobility, a theme which emerges powerfully in "The Master," a poem on Lincoln in *The Town Down the River*. That citizen applied to Lincoln "our shopman's test of age and worth," not seeing that the test of a true citizen is his capacity to find and promote excellence and virtue, whether he himself possesses these qualities or not. If he cannot do so, then democracy is doomed.

The theme that we find thus early in the poetry and which is one with the theme of failure and hidden virtue in so many of the early poems comes out strongly in "Cassandra" in *The Man Against the Sky*. America, it seems, feels that God takes care of her as he does drunks and small children: ". . . 'We are young; / O leave us now and let us grow . . .' " But much of the burden of his song has been that time runs out sooner than we think, that "a few complacent years" have made Americans proud and self-deluded. In other words, that European experience the avoidance of which Americans so conspicuously delighted in, which they so arrogantly vilified, and the total absence of which they considered one of the chief of innumerable American virtues, that experience had only been postponed; it would come home with a vengeance. If the Spanish and Mexican wars had shown that America could be as predatory as any empire, World War I, in Robinson's view, would put America on a footing with the other powers, no better indeed and perhaps worse because of its slogans and self-righteousness. "You have the ages for your guide / But not the wisdom to be led."

I think we ought to remember that Robinson was a New Englander of a certain sort—an American, deeply such and the more such for being all unconscious of it. Not for him the intoning of pledges, hymns and liturgies nor paeans to Rockies or whatever; in fact, he thought less than nothing of going out west and looking at phenomena like the Grand Canyon. He took one trip to England, in 1923, which for old New Englanders of his sort was far more logical than going to Texas and vastly more rewarding for a literary man, or so he would naturally have thought; East meant more than West and those who went West went because they couldn't make it back East. England was delightful in many ways, particularly London, literary London, though he was appalled by the garrulity of the Oxford and London intellectuals and literati. After six weeks he came home, turned up at Peterborough and told Mrs. Mac-Dowell that he had "weighed two things—England's hedges and New England's stone walls. And I found I cared more for the stone walls." He did not resent the English nor feel inferior nor find them cold; indeed it appears he felt quite at ease with them and on at least one occasion probably talked more, consecutively and easily, than he had done in years, and this among writers like Galsworthy and John Drinkwater. That is understandable; he was *primus inter pares,* a notable foreign poet, accepted for who he was and what he had done. No need to hide or to fear self-betrayal under such circumstances. He might well have stayed to be lionized, and the sequel will show that he did not wholly object to discreet admiration. The impulse to return home must owe something to a kind of New England parochialism that is at once the vice as it is the virtue of its character and art. He belonged at home, that's all, and home now meant Peterborough and Monadnock. He was simply homesick. He felt deeply the pull of his blood and imagination towards England and the great literary dead, his forebears poetic and ancestral, but New England was nearer still, his people had been there three centuries, and at his age what had "travel" as such to teach him? Besides, in England there were no rocking chairs. He would have agreed with Hawthorne that his plot of New England was about as much as his heart could take in. Any suggestion that New England was not "typically American" would have called up a flare of that temper rarely evoked but well noticed when it appeared. He loved his country —his part of it—and the more deeply because he had concentrated both the area and the love. He had hoped to see a nation, a republic, that grew nobler, more civilized but believed he saw a mobocracy increasingly dominated by and directed towards money and power.

William Vaughn Moody, Robinson's fellow poet and sometime rival as well as friend, had already shown the United States of the Spanish War and the Philippine adventure as a nation in the process of becoming an imperialist power—as in fact betraying its true purpose of giving to the world a hope for better things by way of an idealism, generosity and truly democratic spirit which should be the last best hope of men all over the world. Though no Moody and no Walt Whitman, Robinson clearly held views that, though moderate and sober as we might expect, still had in them something at once of the New England transcendental and of what he called in *Captain Craig* the "triumphant and American." In that passage he writes of a putative poet who dreams of a great American epic; in "The White Lights" he celebrated Moody's *The Great Divide* and again in the context of the Greek and Roman republics. "No prophet knew from what was done / That there was triumph in the air." "The White Lights" ends thus. The note, triumphant, American, comes from the two greatest civilizations he knew of, the British and the Roman, direct to the civilization in the making which, honoring its ancestry, yet aimed to go further and higher. If Robinson sounded his own warning note, and he was by no means alone in doing so, he may well have sounded it more from native caution than from profound insight into the hidden dynamism of American "progress." Yet we cannot doubt his misgivings as the century advanced; their expression finds voice first in "The Master" in *The Town Down the River*, a poem which, though "supposed to have been written not long after the Civil War," as the note to the poem puts it, has direct reference to the temper of the time in the first decade of this century. Like Whitman, Robinson sees Lincoln as larger than life, as the complete democrat who yet is among the "kings of earth," an "Olympian," a "Titan." The failure of Lincoln's task is our failure as men and citizens: he was the great teacher and we would not learn; he loved greatly and we paid no heed; he saw the truth and we looked elsewhere. In essence, both Whitman and Robinson seem to conclude that Americans have not proved worthy of their heroes, and the hero of heroes is Lincoln. The penalty we shall pay comes straight from our "fond self-shadowings / Wherewith we cumber the Unknown . . ." In the end, we shall pay for that self-indulgent neglect of teaching and example. We shall "flourish in our perigee," but it is the low point, nevertheless.

The note sounds in some of the poems of the next volume, *The Man Against the Sky*, rather crudely in "Cassandra," with great delicacy in "Hillcrest"; Robinson was no better than most poets at the "public," occasional poem. But the themes of decay, breakup, of spoiled success and redeemed failure sound far more insistently and will loom larger and larger in the two Arthurian poems, *Merlin* (1917) and *Lancelot* (1920). Both are "about" the War, avowedly so; Robinson knew from the start that America could not keep out of the mess, if only because it had lost the power, the virtue, to cast off the last traces of its European provenience and move directly towards its truest goal, which was that of becoming itself. The central corruption which Europe cannot escape, which is her destiny, America might have escaped, once; now America, still a part of the Old World, must be dragged down with it—or, just possibly, may by learning to see, as Lincoln tried to teach it to see, face the true knowledge of its destiny and in finally striving towards it, save not only the New World but redeem the Old as well.

The notion has a familiar ring; we still hear it from time to time and it echoes quaintly down the past. Robinson, a man too disenchanted ever to grow cynical, knew how hollow the old hortatory and inspirational folklore had become; indeed, he shows some exemplary models in a few poems, models of the American, early twentieth-century urban type. Essentially, he sees him as con man, whether ultimately "successful" or the contrary. "Bokardo," which Chard Powers Smith considers a portrait of Herman Robinson, and "Old Trails," a far better poem, represent this exemplary mode. In the first case, the man addressed has followed the typical American entrepreneurial pattern; in the second, we find a man who *knows* he will "make it" granted the right admixture of luck and timing. He has to wait, but all things are added unto him: ". . . Three years he toiled / In Yonkers, and then sauntered into fame."

Again and again, critics have spoken of Robinson's attacks on American "materialism" and venality, if you like. True, he does inveigh against these things, but I believe they bother him not so much in themselves as because they represent a deep American failing: the inability to aim high and to respect those who do, unless that aim works, and works for conspicuous worldly success, which means money and economic power. Lincoln ultimately fails because we did not know what he was up to and still do not—never will, in fact, the poet implies. Greatness is a conception we as Americans simply cannot believe in; Robinson says it plainly in a very mediocre poem on Theodore Roosevelt, "The Revealer," in *The Town Down the River*. An exercise in enforced piety, enforced by the poet's sense of obligation to the President who had given him help in time of need, it ends this volume as "The Master" begins it. The former clearly states the thematic connection between the two, and it ends with the contemptuous dismissal of Americans as essentially blind, lost in a mistaken view of our destiny and the nature of humanity. We had as a gift a leader who released us from error, from the prison of our delusion; we have to "see," we have to take advantage of what the great men who sometimes spring up among us can do to make us free. But in the long run we have to want freedom and to persist after the great man of the hour has departed. Robinson says here and elsewhere that we never have, never will.

The Robinson who thus expresses disillusion with the progress of American democracy is one with the poet who feels that the materialism which afflicts society derives from science, or more properly, scientism. That he stood in awe of much science and technology we can tell from some of the letters as well as from certain poems. He often takes a Romantic view of science, seeing in it the Faustian overreacher and at the same time the possibility of a kind of redemption. In one of his letters he expresses the view that orthodox religion is dead and that the vacuum thus left only science can fill, which it is just about getting ready to do. With his nineteenth-century New England appetite for the metaphysical and transcendental he could not settle for the kind of existential grind he knew at first hand. Just because he had lived it, did that make it True in the larger sense? The only sense that counts? Much as we may be convinced of Robinson's realism and his disenchanted view of existence, the other side of his nature—what Kipling called "the separate sides of my head"—yearned for a grand synthesis, a key to all mythologies, an "orient Word." If none existed, then someone would have to make it up, and at least in certain contexts he seemed to think that science could provide the necessary way towards belief and certitude.

In "The Man Against the Sky" Robinson was not yet ready

to accept the possibility of a scientific grand synthesis; he still remains in the position of Arnold, of most nineteenth-century poets and intellectuals, between worlds and full of uncertainty, seeing the scientific spirit as largely destructive and providing nothing to replace the faith and morality it has destroyed. Robinson being a New Englander and the man he was, he could not share Arnold's curiously naïve view of Poetry as a religion; the very best he could do was to assert the primacy of the spiritual in the face of materialism. Since he had lived by that assertion and had come through a very bitter ordeal in so living, he had to feel that his very survival as man and poet testified to the validity of his creed. He had proved it in action. "The Man Against the Sky" declares, among other things, that a man can outface all doubts and all "facts" denying the spiritual if he will "go forward like a stoic Roman," as "Hillcrest" shows that men can see the truth of themselves and survive—as long as they know they do not live in "a world without meaning." The split between the spiritual and material realms which the later nineteenth century saw widen to an impassable gulf very nearly swallowed up not only Robinson but poetry and the arts. Much has been made—indeed it forms a major part of the thesis of W. R. Robinson's book—of the philosophical effort to join once again these two realms of flesh and spirit and of Robinson's recasting of his beliefs in the light of his own thought. Mr. Robinson says, "Much more philosophically inclined than Howells . . . Robinson abandoned the inadequate attitudes deriving from materialism and emerged not an antirealist but a realist of a more profound kind." Very true, yet it really begs the question, for what does "profound" mean? I suggest that it means what in a really fine poet it is bound to mean: he lived in his time and generation and he felt the temper of both in his blood and nerves. And of course one man's reality is another man's illusion. Robinson was faithful to life as he saw and experienced it. He wrote about the way things looked and he took pains to get the actuality of the look so that there might be a surface clear enough to see through. Yet the surface must be there. He would have agreed with Blake that "Eternity is in love with the productions of Time."

None of these remarks means to suggest that Robinson wrote

ignorantly about merely everyday grimness. The point remains that he had very little formal training in philosophical and scientific thought and, indeed, confessed himself incapable of grasping what Royce said in lecture. But this assumes that poets and people in general learn chiefly from classes, lectures and textbooks. They don't of course, and Robinson was, like Dryden and Kipling, one of those who pick up things in conversation, liked to hear others talk their "shop" and remembered what they said. Robinson over the years constantly associated with men like Louis and Burnham and Saben who, while failures as economic products, had brilliant intellects and knew a great deal. Night after night in the Village and in Boston and Peterborough he sat silent and heard people talk. What he learned about ideas and about those who held them and held forth about them the poems can largely display. One of the best examples, though it deals chiefly with the man and not so much with his ideas, is "The Wandering Jew," that superb portrait of the intellectual who wills his blindness and illusion. How sardonically Robinson speaks of himself as bringing "the tribute of a tempered ear / To an untempered eloquence." We have all known such men and such nights, of brilliant talk, vague and bombastic rhetoric, jargon, half-drunken insights! Here, outlasting all, is the man of the fixed idea, the half-mad and obsessed prophet of doom. What Robinson sees, notably, is the man's wholly irrelevant and outdated concern and obsession; what he anathematizes has long since ceased to plague the world, at least in the form he gives to it. The figure Robinson uses to express the evils the old man inveighs against is that of

> New lions ramping in his path.
> The old were dead and had no fangs
> Wherefore—he loved them—seeing not
> They were the same that in their time
> Had eaten everything they caught.

How human the old man is and how familiar, under the guise of any religious or sacramentally held political faith. The question that I seek to resolve, rather than answer, is: Does Robinson have a close relationship to the scientific and philosophical thought of his time? If one means by the question, did he have a reasoned position which weighed ideas and made conclusions on the basis of the weighing, the answer must be negative. If on the other hand we ask whether he was aware of much of the main current of ideas in his age, I think we can say yes, provided we understand that the awareness remains just that: not an intellectual position, no philosophy of life or thought or art, no epistemology, but a set of responses and feelings and temperamental inclinations. The Robinson who wrote *King Jasper* (1935) takes a far different view of life from the poet of *Captain Craig*. He came a long way, and if "The Man Against the Sky" marks the end of one kind of thinking about the unthinkable, *King Jasper* in some sense points in the direction he would have gone had he lived.

The philosopher who would seem to have the most in common with Robinson is William James. Not only do the two share a certain tentativeness of approach to their investigations, but both include oppositions and paradox and rest their cases on the experience lived and the idea made flesh before it returns again to idea. Pragmatism certainly marks the best of Robinson's poetry. Again and again the characters in his poems prove the truth or falsehood of their feelings and beliefs with their blood, so to speak. Robinson sets experience, and truth to it, as the one valid test. But beyond that still shines the transcendent which cannot change. Though the woman of "Eros Turannos" must know there is a way out, such a way cannot be for her. Nor does the speaker of "Hillcrest," though convinced of his smallness and unwisdom, deny that size and wisdom exist. Robinson's own experience taught him that the spiritual realm lives and that the material lives only to serve it. In effect what begins with Robinson in assertion ends with the certitude that a man must "get used to not getting used," which is after all as good a description of life as any. Above all, he must pityingly reject the Wandering Jew because he will not learn from experience: in his anger, learning and vehemence simply "relegate him out of time / To chaos . . ." Robinson knew well the doctrinaire, fanatic types that haunt intellectual Bohemia and who, like the anarchists of Conrad's *Secret Agent,* lose their own humanity and sacrifice that of others in the name of their ideas. Such men are mad and all times and places know them:

> And somewhere among men today
> Those old, unyielding eyes may flash
> And flinch—and look the other way.

Illusion can kill and it can save. Robinson like William James allows for "varieties of religious experience."

By 1917 the unspeakable carnage of the war must have come home in some measure to the consciousness of all reasonable men. Yet even then few could see how the horror began or how it could be ended. Such a time could not be called auspicious for poetry; no wonder Yeats responded as he did to a request for a war poem. For Robinson, now in his late forties, the spectacle of this abomination, while it did not surprise, could certainly daunt. *Merlin,* very quickly followed by *Lancelot* in point of composition, shows the strategy he employed for dealing once again with the themes of breakup and chaos which had for so long concerned him. And he starts with the strategy not of symbol or allegory, but of analogy. The failure of Camelot, of the Round Table, is Arthur's failure. An entire generation or cadre of leaders had failed the nation and betrayed the realm. The wisest abdicate their responsibilities; the brave give way to the untrustworthy, and so on. Not a remarkable insight, we might think, and indeed its very ordinariness of approach puts it in the category of what one might term the Robinsonian fictional realism. Intent as he is throughout the Arthurian trilogy on demythologizing the stories he uses, he rather seems to attempt a kind of Meredithian fiction which still aims at something like tragedy, though with a certain amount of humor and in a low key. Robinson has been taken to task by a number of critics for emptying the stories of their mythical content, and I think their case against his strategy is a strong one. Yet we should understand why he adopted it, what he was after, positively as well as negatively. In the latter case, he had simply had enough of late nineteenth-century mythologizing. True child of the realist movement, he could see such matters as the love potion in the Tristram story as mere hocus-pocus; how could one believe such stuff in this enlightened age? That he missed the point many critics have been eager to demonstrate. Yet if we grant his aims as a narrative poet, then we must debate the matter further. Robinson does not here deal in myth, symbol and allegory. Analogy is what concerns him, and analogy implies, I think, the use of a story, of whatever provenience, as a method of distancing a contemporary problem, dilemma or catastrophe.

Lancelot, Guenevere, Arthur, Merlin, Vivian: all the chief characters of the trilogy represent for Robinson people who, while characteristically modern, reach back into time and hence display abiding human dilemmas. The Great War prompted him to look for correspondences, for an oblique view of the contemporary. The trouble comes, really, from a kind of dislocation: just as these folk are not the men and women of the myth, the larger-than-life archetypes we can accept in all their profound simplicity and vitality, so also do they fail to touch our contemporary sense of what is actual, "real"; they remain literary, fabrications, creatures of Robinson's own fancy, perhaps based on his own experience of certain sophisticated demimondaine types, the rich and near-rich, but certainly creatures of words and words alone, it sometimes seems. George Meredith looms behind many of the narrative poems, and nowhere larger—nor indeed more successfully—than in *Merlin*. Both Meredith and Robinson understood something that was not often adverted to in the literature of their time: the complexity of, and the necessity for, establishing a new relationship between the sexes. I suspect that Meredith's *Modern Love* had as great an effect on Robinson as did the novels. Surely the declaration that "we are betrayed by what is false within" finds many changes rung upon it in the long poems. In *Merlin* and *Lancelot*, though the relationships between men and women have as much meaning for Arthur's realm as for the husbands, wives and lovers as individuals, the emphasis remains personal; Robinson, here as elsewhere, shows the woman as never truly found by her lover, as one who suffers or endures while fully understanding the man in the case. In such poems as "John Gorham," "The Unforgiven," (which seems to put a case for divorce), "Ben Trovato," "The Book of Annandale" or "Mortmain," the theme is that of the wife or woman who endures the thoughtless disregard of a husband or lover, the woman who, taken for granted, either finally breaks or goes on enduring. Robinson apparently sometimes spoke of the superior humanity of women, and he obviously despised the "double standard" which involves among other things the right of man to ignore woman and the duty of woman to sacrifice to and for man. The attitude goes deep in his experience. Perhaps a kind of reverence for woman-kind both protected him from them and attracted them to him, as attracted they indeed were. But more than anything else, I think, Robinson shows the inhumanity of indifference, of treating others as conveniences, as things. In "John Gorham" we see a poem which corresponds closely to Henry James's "The Beast in the Jungle." Jane Wayland says to John Gorham, "Somewhere in me there's a woman, if you know the way to find her," and the line might serve as an epigraph to the James story. Like Meredith, Robinson saw all relationships between men and women as shifting, possibly stormy, always requiring both active participation and growth. John Gorham cannot grow as James's Marcher cannot, but whereas Meredith sees women as in their own ways as proud and as capable of coldness as men, Robinson nearly always finds the man guilty of the indifference, abstractness or inaction that brings the tragedy. He insists upon the moral imperative of action, which means growth and change —"steps to the great place."

There is another side to the affair. Actions may be public or private, but feelings must remain of the latter sort. The inner self must open out to another, and if fidelity is to have depth it must remain singular. In "A Tree in Pamela's Garden" or in "Vain Gratuities," as far more strikingly and profoundly in "Eros Turannos," the world outside has its views and makes its false judgment. Whether or not the outside world is correct in its interpretation of "the story of a house" we can never decide, since we can never know that story, nor can the outside world do more than engage in speculation which may amuse or hurt, but never comprehend, the principals. Always Robinson insists on the comprehension, the understanding, or as he would say, the "seeing," because only such understanding or vision can bring about right action, which is the aim. Although few of Robinson's long poems deal with dramatic action, all derive from specific actions in the past by the principals and move toward an action, or act, in the moral and spiritual spheres which shall determine, release, restore or ruin. People in Robinson's poems are continually talking, trying to make feeling, action and thought coalesce. At times they ruminate, but for the most part they speak to others or rather another, in a kind of public speech which is yet meant for a private audience. True, Robinson will ruminate, mumble and divagate into over-qualification of an exasperating kind, but he does not, like Pound or Stevens, address himself or nobody. Robinson has some kind of audience before him, as Browning does, and most novelists. I think that approach in part explains why we cannot ever lose ourselves in a Robinson long narrative: both he and we always remain too conscious of one another's presence, and the poet seems to think he must constantly entertain us with elaborate jokes, sleights of language, tricky comparisons, paradoxes: ". . . and the whole house / Was like a thing alive only with dying." This, from *Cavender's House,* is wholly typical. One could make an interminable list of just that kind of trick, which though sometimes neat and effective in context, more often becomes mechanical, show-off, irritating. And more than anything else, the tricks don't get us anywhere. When Robinson writes a story poem, long or short, he is best when he moves in on his plot in the Jamesian manner; when the manner is Meredithian, we are all in trouble.

These matters bear importantly on the Arthurian poems, but most of all on *Tristram,* the longest, in its time the most successful by far, and to the modern reader the least rewarding, I think. Of the three, *Merlin* seems to me the most entertaining; the scenes between Merlin and Vivian have wit, high color, and a sense of actuality. Vivian in particular comes alive in all her beauty, wit, duplicity and simple bitchiness—a most feminine and appealing character, if you like them that devastating. But she is a worthy mate for Merlin, who it sometimes seems has too portentous a load to carry, as poetic device, to become as real as Vivian does. In much the same way, Guenevere is a more impressive figure than either Arthur or even Lancelot, who overshadows the rest. In effect, Robinson cannot handle a stageful of persons; like many an amateur dramatist, he gets people on stage but finds most of them supernumerary and can't think how to get them off. His best scenes are dialogues, like those between Merlin and Vivian, or that between Lancelot and Guenevere in the convent at Almesbury. Chard Powers Smith may well be right in asserting that Guenevere was drawn from the life, was Robinson's great love; when his women have any life at all, they have vastly more than the men and give off an atmosphere of vitality, passion and generosity of heart and spirit the men usually lack. The scheme holds good in short poems as well as long. When he hits his stride in opposing a man and a woman, he can write with economy, wit and a nervous, sinewy rhythm, as in the scenes just mentioned. I think most readers would agree that *Tristram* fails because the passion of the lovers lacks actuality; it must be shown and Robinson does not show it, whereas Isolt of Brittany has some degree of reality because she bears the stamp, to some extent, of a Robinsonian "failure."

It was like that
For women, sometimes,
For women like her. She hoped there were not many
Of them, or many of them to be, not knowing
More about that than about waves and foam,
And white birds everywhere, flying, and flying;
Alone, with her white face and her gray eyes,
She watched them there till even her thoughts were white
And there was nothing alive but white birds flying,
Flying, and always flying, and still flying,
And the white sunlight flashing on the sea.

In her childlike, rather pallid, devotion to Tristram, as man and as memory, she touches us far more nearly than her rival and "successful" namesake, whose passional nature we have to accept as given. Robinson attempts a kind of Wagnerian crescendo, an orgasmic or at any rate sexual surging which strikes one as a trifle embarrassing, I think. He isn't the type, really, we feel, and though he loved Wagner's operas, notably *Tristan*, he could not achieve that kind of magnificent vulgarity himself. His lovers remain eminently civilized folk who surely love and die and so forth, but not to Wagnerian trombones; after all, Captain

Craig's own last and typically sardonic word was "trombones."

I do not believe Robinson makes enough out of his use of the myths to warrant all the paraphernalia required. It would have been more economical to have given us a realistic narrative about contemporary men and women and events, though he wanted the myth for reasons of analogy and reference. Yet to demythologize his basic plot and fabric was a fatal flaw: either the story must go from everyday—or at any rate, accepted—actuality to symbolic gesture and evocation, or it must grow from the mythical, the unconscious perhaps, towards the affairs of living men and women in a living world. These poems take neither course. We cannot accept them as natural emanations from the past, the profound, the evocative, nor can we see any more relevance to the lives of people living in the earlier decades of this century than the general notion of worlds breaking up and the death of God and so forth. Robinson does not give his actors anything to *do*. By omitting, for example, the fact of Excalibur and its physical as well as metaphysical being, of Camelot sustained by the harmonious music that built it, of indeed the whole *company* of the Table Round and all the trappings of the story, he deprives it of vitality. Paradoxically, because he wishes to make it credible, we cannot believe in it. He could not see that to remove what he called "the fool potion" was to remove the genesis of power, to deprive the tale of its furious passion which is the whole point: "C'est Vénus toute entière à sa proie attachée." Of course, he did not want that kind of thing, yet he does in fact seem to try for it in *Tristram,* but having eliminated the possibility of action by eliminating the love-potion, he might far better have stayed away from the story altogether. It is a story of Possession. He could do it himself in "Luke Havergal," "Eros Turannos," "The Gift of God," but in those poems he fitted subject, theme, setting and tone to his own best gift. *Tristram* has neither the genuine lyricism nor the effective dialogues of *Merlin* and *Lancelot.* It came from his will, not his imagination.

Yet what are these Arthurian poems about and why did he write them? The last question is the more easily answered, I think, and perhaps in a single word: Anti-Romanticism, a kind of Shavian impulse to disinfect human love of illusion and bar-

barism and to turn it calm, reasonable, safe. For all his preoc-
cupation with the vicissitudes of love and passion, he would
have agreed that "men have died and worms have eaten them /
But not for love . . ." One endures and takes whatever medicine
provided. At the end of *Tristram* the lovers understand and forgive and accept because they know that they were immoderate,
possessive and wrong, just as Lancelot knows that he has done
wrong and goes forth to find the "Light." Robinson wrote these
tales of passion out into civilized dialogues in order to show
himself, if no one else, that love wrongly placed is analogous to
any other misplaced or misdirected passion, ambition, or desire:
it holds within itself the power to stand for all human striving.
And since for Robinson to fail while gaining understanding was
far nobler than to succeed while going blind, the stories become
for him exemplary, like so many of his other poems, of the belief in going from strength to strength. As "The Man Against
the Sky" proves, he believed that suicide was the only right
response to a disbelief in life after death. To attain to a convinced acceptance of immortality comes hard; men must fight
to believe, not wait for the "spark from heaven to fall" like
Arnold's scholar-gipsy. Robinson wrote *Merlin* and *Lancelot* because he deeply felt the exigency of his own need to "see" and
to put down what he saw.

The poems are of course about love, love and war or love and
hatred. Neither is possible without the other, or perhaps we
might say that a kind of dynamic tension between the two
makes the true civilized time and person. So in his failure Merlin sees that there is "a cold angel" called "Change" and a Fate
which even God cannot alter. When people do not see, do not
put themselves in harmony with true change and destiny, then
love becomes hatred, peace war. Reasonable, civilized men and
women can not so much subdue passion as control it, make it
run deep rather than wide, and always remember that they may
be wrong. Not all the world loves a lover; love can make the
world go wrong; love can make war. Like so many of the late
long poems, these three deal with men and women who see too
little and too late, but in most cases are redeemed by an understanding acceptance after their worlds have been shattered. In
this trilogy, war and the breaking of nations provide the back-

ground for blind, selfish or betrayed love. As Dagonet tells
Gawaine in *Merlin*, all the cross-currents of misapplied, because
misunderstood, feeling mean violence, war. And in the midst of
all this passionate hate, love and ambition, "There's a squeezed
world that elbows for attention." Civilization gets short shrift
while all these passionate heroes and heroines have their high
old times. Ordinary folk just go out and get killed by order.
Merlin and Vivian can go in for dalliance, but they do so at
everyone else's expense. Merlin should read the fate of the king-
dom, advise the king, set things right or try to do so. He pre-
fers Vivian, an eminently understandable attitude, but the consequence of it is the loss of the realm and Vivian too. Every
one of the major actors plays the fool except the Fool, who
cannot act but only speak.

Tristram, as we have seen, presents a rather different aspect,
though it too deals with hate and love and the suggested reconciliation of both at last. The poem is half again as long as
Merlin or *Lancelot*, the characters have less to do and there are
fewer of them. None is as interesting as Vivian; even Isolt of
Brittany who, though by far the most attractive, has little
depth. The two earlier poems do get at a valid theme and make
it seem important intermittently; I find *Tristram* a weary poem
and one which seems written for a woman's magazine of the
time, or as close to that as Robinson could get, and there is
some evidence to suggest that he intended the poem to be a
popular success, almost on a dare. He wrote perhaps rather
shamefacedly to Emma Robinson that he was getting "a lot of
unwholesome publicity over *Tristram*." It would appear that he
himself thought less of the poem than of either of the other
parts of the trilogy, but he said in the same letter to Emma
that "it's 'all about love' and that seems to be what people
want . . ." For once he had set out to make a "popular" success and had indeed succeeded. Those readers of the poetry
who had always liked to "make romance of reticence," as "The
Tree in Pamela's Garden" has it, naturally saw *Tristram* as
autobiographical and a full account of the poet's great and only
love, a flight of fancy that only goes to show how little they
knew about love, let alone poets. Perhaps the poem has an
element of sexual fantasy; Chard Powers Smith thinks it is

Robinson's account of the "great love" between Herman and Emma, the latter having finally indicated to EA that his brother could never be supplanted in her heart, or something like that. Anyhow, Robinson never did go back to Gardiner after 1925. *Tristram* may in a sense be a farewell to all that.

One quality stands out in the poem: the capacity of the poet to place his sympathy in unlikely quarters. Ultimately, it is the repulsive King Mark who has the last word about the lovers and their "great love." At the end, he sees that a passion of that sort could not be for him. Mark's final soliloquy again reminds of Henry James's Marcher of "The Beast in the Jungle" who comes to know at last what that beast is which will devour him: he would be the one man to whom a great love came and he did not recognize it, he would be that man to whom nothing happened. Robinson may have seen himself, like James perhaps, as the artist who, for all his powers of sympathy and perception, can never truly live the life of passion. Mark can know jealousy, torments of the mind, but he can never lose himself wholly in a transport of feeling. As he says, "there are darknesses / That I am never to know . . ." Here if anywhere lies the autobiographical strain in the poem, in the poet's own confession that great loves and utterly absorbing passions have nothing to do with art. He would have agreed with James that art must be as "hard as nails." And the artist, too?

The Arthurian trilogy, if indeed the term is a proper one, represents for most readers the best of Robinson's narrative— or at any rate long—poems. Between *Merlin* in 1917 and *Tristram* in 1927 are five other books, three of which contain short poems and two which are book-length narratives. *The Three Taverns* (1920) contains at least one of his best poems, "The Wandering Jew," and one of his best monologues, the title poem itself. *Avon's Harvest* (1921) has three of the best sonnets and "Mr. Flood's Party" as well as another fine monologue, "Rembrandt to Rembrandt." *Dionysis in Doubt* (1925) has three or four more excellent sonnets, among them the wry and pungent "New England" and a rather effectively Jamesian dialogue, "Mortmain." After that comes the long twilight of the long poems. *Nicodemus* (1932) is a collection of shorter narrative and dramatic pieces with a couple of rhymed lyrical pieces added. The true lyric vein had run out.

IX

Of Pits Before Him and Of Sands Behind

In 1920, when Robinson had finished *Lancelot,* he had be-hind him seven volumes of poetry. The house of Macmillan thought enough of him to refuse *Lancelot* for publication. The year before, Percy MacKaye had organized a fiftieth birthday celebration for him which made the front page of the New York *Times Book Review.* A number of Robinson's fellow poets wrote tributes, and there can be no doubt that the Festschrift had its practical effect, because in 1921 Macmillan published the first *Collected Poems* and the awards and rewards began to flow in, beginning with the Pulitzer Prize, the first of three he would win before his death. He had indeed "made it"—all the way from rags to, if not riches, solvency. He could pay off his debts over the next few years, live a bit more spaciously, give money to his nieces and to the Gardiner hospital for a laboratory in memory of Dean. But the time had gone by for delight in what the money and fame might do in the way of excitement and new experience. He had never been a man of great vitality and had never been robust; the last years of his life, then, while comfortable, while providing amenities he enjoyed, seem to us prematurely gray and autumnal. He may well have been tired out; many of the letters and poems do give that impression. He lived strenuously and intensely in his art during the four months in Peterborough, but the other eight out of the year almost lack incident altogether. That of course does not mean that nothing happened; perhaps it may signify that he did not grow and change as much as he might have under happier circumstances. Yet he had always been something of a creature of habit, falling quickly into routines as soon as circumstance would allow, and his great loyalty to old friends, notably to Seth Ellis Pope, may have kept him from branching out, from making acquaintances among his literary peers. For example, in 1918 he simply "retired" to Brooklyn to live in a dismal apartment with Pope. That unfortunate, who was one of a number of losers whom Robinson felt for, in part because he knew himself as in some sense a loser too, had reached a low point in a dim career when his wife left him. Robinson, with great charity but what would appear to be a kind of perversity, moved in to cheer his friend up. One may be permitted to doubt that any particular cheer abounded. Yet Robinson defended Pope almost violently; he had very nearly broken with Mrs. Richards when she ventured to suggest that Pope had drawbacks as a schoolteacher. And he flared up whenever anyone hinted that the man was dull and limited, almost as though something crucial to his own self were under attack. He stayed with Pope till the latter's death in 1922, when he moved in with the James Earle Frasers and seemed to join the race and the world of art once again.

Robinson's seeming avoidance of literary men of his own stature may be only seeming. Certainly for most of his productive career he had been passed by in favor of nonentities and sycophants, had seen too many reputations rise and fall to trust the bubble reputation. Still, in the notable cases of Moody and Frost we can see either jealousy or a sense of inadequacy— perhaps both—at work. In the case of Moody, Robinson's attitude was complex, since the men were exact contemporaries and each was conscious of the other as his chief rival for fame, despite the very great difference in their talent. Moody came close to being a genius, so close that he looked more like one than the real thing, and Robinson was taken, and taken in. He admired the man and his—well, not exactly his work, but his poetic being. Moody was all Poet, and Robinson knew only too well how sorry a figure he himself cut in that respect. He felt no jealousy with regard to Moody's poetry but as to Moody's success, that was another matter. At the same time, "The White Lights" exists as evidence of Robinson's generous tribute to the dramatic triumph of Moody's *The Great Divide*, the play that would start a new era in American drama. How many of those plays have been hailed and forgotten? Yet the real fact is that Robinson could not be easy with Moody, as he could not with the editors of the Harvard *Advocate* in his college years, as he could never be easy with the grand "great-house" folk of Gardiner. Why not? As he said, he was "born with his skin inside out," most vulnerable and most sensitive to vulnerability in others. He had seen one of the most admirable of men, his brother Dean, go to pieces while the solid and successful went from strength to strength. When he himself became a success in the twenties and thirties, he apparently went through a brief period of pomposity and arrogance, yet the old self-derogatory irony and the great feeling for others reasserted themselves: when his niece told him that he no longer belonged to the family but to the world, he told her: "I don't think the world is much disturbed about it." That was no pose. Disenchantment had become a poetic strategy and he had come too late to success to be seriously damaged by it. Ultimately, he could not believe in himself as the poet with a capital P, just as he had always felt that someone else, not he, "Long" Robinson, wrote the poetry.

The matter of friendship with other writers of his own stature takes on more meaning in this context. Undoubtedly he assumed that because Moody looked confident and self-possessed he was in fact such. Similarly, he watched the rise of Frost's reputation and apparently wanted Frost to like him and to like his work. Frost must have admired the work—or at any rate up to the point at which it became more politic for him to derogate it. Like Moody, Frost saw Robinson as his greatest rival. Unlike Moody, Frost was not one to tolerate the condition. Robinson had no sense of the politics of art and letters; naïvely, he thought that what counted was good poetry rather than influence in the right quarters. He never really grasped what Frost knew instinctively: in poetry as in anything else, material success comes from being well known, from being a celebrity of a sort. Since most of the influential people who can lift an artist out of obscurity can be got to only by devious ways, none of which have any necessary connection with excellence, a poet must play the political game. All too often, there is, as Lord

Melbourne put it, "no damned nonsense about merit." Frost was a fine poet, but can anyone doubt that mediocrity can do as well in point of fame? Robinson did not know how to begin to "make contacts." He fled from them, in fact. Frost neither liked nor agreed with Pound, but he correctly guessed that Pound was a power and Pound could help him, and he rightly felt that if Pound could get poems published, he, Frost, had a duty to those poems, and he would put up with Pound. Robinson simply could not have done that—in fact, he would very probably have refused to go to see Pound or to see him again if he managed a first visit. A matter of temperament and, possibly, upbringing. Yet when he and Frost met, there was constraint on both sides. That Frost treated Robinson ungenerously the record shows. I do not think that matters as much as the fact that Robinson could not at once reach out to his younger contemporary. Perhaps no one could ever have reached Frost, but did anyone ever reach Robinson? May we not, in effect, be saying that there was no one there to reach in the ordinary sense of the pronoun? Here were two poets, four or more people. What could they ever say to one another?

Robinson felt more at home with friends who in no way rivaled him and who, for all their incapacities and unsuccesses, had simpler, more integrated natures than his own. The poets whom he really knew, men like Ledoux, Torrence and Hagedorn, he could praise, feel at home with, never feel jealous of because they never threatened him as man or poet. They all knew he was the better poet and so did he. He could not have known that they and many others looked on him as a kind of saint. He could feel at ease among the bohemians of the Village of sixty and seventy years ago because they were all losers together, and Robinson, secure with his "demon poesy," as Keats has it, could eke out his marginal existence knowing that the poems would come. He was young, he could stand it, he would go through hell as long as the poems came along in their season.

Season gives way to season. At fifty-two, with a *Collected Poems* and a Pulitzer Prize, something very like fame had come to him, and we might think that ahead lay a period of new growth. In April of 1923 he took his English trip. He had left Brooklyn and Pope's grim quarters to rejoin the life of Manhattan that had always meant so much to him. Peterborough was still an annual fixture for four months. What did he need to set him going again, to open new experience to him? No one can answer the question, if indeed the question has validity at all. Between 1922 and 1925 he rediscovered the sonnet, wrote half a dozen of his finest; he also set, in *Roman Bartholow* (1923), a pattern for the long blank verse poem that he would follow more and more as the years went by. But the following year he published *The Man Who Died Twice* which, along with *Amaranth* (1934), rises above the almost undifferentiated level of the rest of the long poems. He had over the years left literary developments and movements entirely alone and in fact read nothing in poetry but his own work. His case is not unique. In his later years Yeats read his own work almost exclusively. Wallace Stevens seems to have been unaware that there was any poetry other than his own. Certain critics have taken Robinson to task for his failure to retool, as it were, to check the latest breakthroughs and go mod. Art—literary art, or at any rate, poetry—does not work that way, which may in part explain why it is never popular in the popular sense. Robinson had to write in order to be assured of his own existence, but he also had to write in order to keep writing. He observed that "a poet who has stopped writing is just an old man and he can't be helped." He did not intend to stop and would "turn things out once a year as long as they want me to." From, roughly, the time of *Tristram* to the last two years of his life, he composed long poem after long poem, nine in all between 1923 and the end in 1935. The mere feat itself seems remarkable. Yet today a reader may well ask what value all these pages of identical-seeming verse may retain. The question needs asking and as full an answer as may profit readers and Robinson alike.

In the first place, the poems are not quite as uniformly colorless and routine as might seem. *Tristram* in fact goes in pretty strongly for the purple patch and lyric flight, not necessarily to the poem's advantage. Weariness seems to creep into many of the works—weariness and a tendency towards archness, circumlocutory and periphrastic witticism, elaborateness of expression for its own sake. The tendency towards self-parody that has been the bane of most American writers—James, Whitman, Faulkner, Hemingway—afflicted Robinson. These endless tales of triangles and spiritual rebirth or death or both or whatnot appear to us too often as one interminable, gray poem. Yet he wore himself out over them, caught up in the involutions of his own rhetoric and as trapped there as ever James was in his. And yet . . . *The Man Who Died Twice,* published in 1924, has subdued power and a real relevance. It may have its *longueurs* but very few, and it deals with some of Robinson's central themes: art, failure, self-knowledge. Ten years later, the year before his death, he published another variation on that theme, *Amaranth.* These two in their quiet way extend the range of the long poem and must certainly be among the few long poems of the century with power to survive. Neither deals with love and eternal triangles; both come fairly directly out of the poet's own life and experience.

Fernando Nash, of *The Man Who Died Twice,* is a composer who "had it—once," had it and let it go until it escaped him forever. A man endowed with a genius that was the envy and scorn of his contemporaries, he failed to use his gift, squandered his power in drink and "lust." Now, at the end, alone, sick and dying, with a failed life and a ruined genius behind him, he waits for the end and for the magnificent music which he will hear at the end and which he might once have composed had he learned to "wait" and to accede to the demands of his genius and his God. And as he has burned his three abortive symphonies, so at the end the narrator has Fernando's body burned at his request and the ashes sunk in the sea. Similarly, the Fargo of *Amaranth,* ten years after renouncing art to become a "mender of pumps," returns in a vision to that "lost world" or "wrong world" where wander the self-deluded and futile "artists" who have neither talent nor honesty and who, under the gaze of Amaranth, "the flower that never fades," turn to a little mound of dust. In *The Man Who Died Twice,* the failed, spoiled genius of Fernando Nash quails before the picture of "the competent plain face of Bach / Calm in achievement . . ." What Fernando Nash threw away out of an obscure self-destructiveness, the characters in *Amaranth* falsely assume to be their birthright. As they go on grinding out "works of art," secure in their achieved blindness, so Fernando, facing death and the full realization of his betrayal of a great gift, accepts the justice of his fate and saves his soul, whereas there may be some doubt as to the existence of a soul in such a character as Miss Watchman or "Pink the poet" or indeed the whole strange crew of self-deceiving artists in *Amaranth*—except Fargo, who after ten years of delusion faces the truth at last and finds the courage to go on past suicide to useful life in a real world.

The correspondences are many, obviously. But more than that, both poems are interesting because they deal with important themes deeply felt by Robinson. *The Man Who Died Twice* is the more compact of the two, but *Amaranth* creates an extraordinary hallucinated world that seems part bohemian underground and part ruined port city so characteristic of New England, and the whole nightmare scene in its muted way evokes echoes of other and earlier poems such as "Luke Havergal" and "Eros Turannos." The place is hell of a kind; the ruined wharves and the black water, the ships, the ghosts and the atmosphere of claustrophobia combine to conjure up Robinson's Gardiner, the Gardiner that was the stage of Herman's defeat and Dean's disintegration. There can be no coincidence in the dedication of this poem: "To the Memory of H. Dean Robinson." If ever a man found himself in "the wrong world," it was Dean. Yet despite the seeming grimness of theme, setting and story, the poem has a kind of joy running subtly through it, and indeed it ends on such a note, one not merely of calm acceptance or stoic resignation, but of joy. The real world returns to Fargo and he to it, to "sunlight and deliverance" and "the sound of living." And instead of the triangle we have a cast of fine, seedy bohemians and failed professionals of many sorts, as well as touches of real wit rather than the tiresome archness that the weary poet labored in many of the long poems. Ampersand, the cat in *Amaranth,* could so easily have become a piece of whimsy; Robinson makes a neat, witty character of him. There is no fuss made. The absurd, menacing and sad jostle one another; characters disappear or dwindle to a pile of dust. One half suspects a few are would-be artists of the poet's own acquaintance. But nowhere do we find malice, bitterness or sentimentality.

What I have been saying may persuade the reader that at

the very end of his career and life, Robinson felt an upsurge of the old spirit. *Talifer* (1933), the predecessor of *Amaranth,* may be the very worst poem he ever wrote, and of course coming as it does after a number of increasingly abstruse and attenuated long poems, it can have the effect of killing off interest in the last two narratives. Most of all, the reiteration of the blank verse line may well deaden a reader's perception, simply get between him and the text. Yet I believe that both *Amaranth* and *King Jasper* do things with blank verse that Robinson had never done before. He runs his lines on far more effectively; he roughens the line, finds more resources in the verse-paragraph. Much derives from a new terseness and economy of style. He embarks on an epigram, makes the point and leaves it, without the long embellishment, the elaboration. *King Jasper* he wrote when he was dying, really, and no one would call it a success, yet again there are interesting things about it, not the least of which is the versification. I do not think many readers today will be persuaded by Robinson's allegory of capitalism, communism, democracy. Yet the poem touches on another theme of real importance in his work: America and its mission of hope for the future. Again and again he had returned to the problems of democracy and of reconciling materialism and power with the spiritual. We got the first sense of his American-ness in *Captain Craig* and now at the very end, thinly veiled by the allegory, he comes to what we might call a full-scale consideration of the fate of industrialized American democracy under extremes of pressure from left and right. The poem fails: *Amaranth* has more ease, variety, wit and grace, but Robinson was a dying man, in pain often and very weak when he pushed ahead with *King Jasper.* He really seems despite illness to have found something new. Certainly the lyric impulse had departed, as he confessed himself, but the persistence with which he pressed on in long poems might have, had he lived, cleared a way for a renascence. In any case, persistence made *Amaranth* possible, and for that we can be grateful.

The last ten years of Robinson's life saw him in fairly steady progress from New York to Boston to Peterborough and back again. He continued to live with the Frasers in New York, in a newly remodeled house near the East River on 42nd Street.

They were years of increasing triumph for him, particularly when *Tristram* came out in 1927, was adopted by the Literary Guild, and he became a literary lion, with a public reception at the Little Theater complete with a reading from the poem by Mrs. August Belmont. *Tristram* won him a third Pulitzer *(The Man Who Died Twice* won his second in 1923) and the money— the real stuff—began to come in handsomely, and he could pay off the last of his debts; more important, he could give real help to others. He was Somebody. Even Gardiner had to acknowledge that he was her most famous son. It was a kind of subtle revenge he could not have failed to enjoy, though he did not ever really dwell on such affairs. What bothered him most was the seemingly excessive element in the reception accorded *Tristram.* He knew it wasn't that good. He knew, in fact, that no good poetry is that kind of good. He went up to Peterborough and started to write again.

At the Colony he was the uncrowned king; in a real sense the place centered itself upon him. Every newcomer got instruction as to the observances appropriate to the Great Poet. A reader today may be pardoned for a certain impatience with such reverential behavior. And indeed among the younger and rising poets and critics the reaction had already set in. Robinson's triumphs and successes had never really touched the newer postwar generation of writers and critics. If one looks at the list of poets who came to his fiftieth anniversary observance one remembers the names, indeed they are period pieces, but one knows nothing of their work any more, with the isolated exception of an isolated poem by three or four of them; which is only to say that Robinson remained marginal always, never entered the arena of reputation-making, and though he seemed at last to have reached an unassailable position, that was illusion: those who made much of him and his work were neither the makers nor the arbiters of the new poetry. When Eliot observed that Robinson's work was "negligible" he spoke literal truth: Eliot and the others could and did neglect that work because it had never really reached them and by now the mainstream had diverged. In the early days of Robinson's fame, reviewers would group him with Lindsay, Markham, and Masters; today he stands alone. The others we do not read and never will. He happened in a time that saw the beginning of an extraordinarily rich literary period in American literature. He did most of his best work before it began and when it reached its peak he was never associated with it since he knew practically none of the shapers of the age and they did not read him and could not know their real kinship with him. And as the younger men came along, many naturally assumed that the author of the late long poems was the essential poet; what did they know of the great lyrics and the dramatic pieces? He was the pop poet of *Tristram* and of tricks like "Richard Cory."

If the miserable misunderstanding with Frost is any test, it can be assumed that Robinson did not enjoy the position, that he understood that it was so but could not see how or why it had happened. He went his rounds from New York to Boston where he stayed several weeks with his old friend Burnham, as he had stayed so long with Pope in Brooklyn. Then to Peterborough and the four months at hard labor. New York in fact had become too exhausting for him, particularly after his work in Peterborough. He wanted to be near his friends, but more and more he dreaded the literary tea fights and such. It seems, really, that what he needed and wanted was a home of his own and someone to take care of him. The list of those who wanted to take him in included his niece, Ruth Nivison of Gardiner, but he would not go back there; he wanted "a safer way / Than growing old alone among the ghosts," as he wrote in "Old Trails." He never went to Tilbury Town after his farewell to the "ghosts" in 1925, coincident with his being "doctored," as he put it, by Bowdoin College. Perhaps it was too painful to go there, but just as likely he had had enough—Gardiner simply did not mean that much; Emma did not need him any more, nor did his nieces, for all their affection. And he needed to be needed. It was during this period, in fact, that he intimated to one or two friends that he might marry and that he was in the market for a wife—nobody in particular, it would seem, but someone who might stabilize his life and solace his loneliness. He cannot have looked forward cheerfully to lonely old age and may well have pondered with some irony his own poem, written many years before, "On the Night of a Friend's Wedding." "If ever I am old and all alone . . ." Friends and admirers stood ready to help him and indeed to spoil him. At least two women whom he had known for some years, Leonora Speyer the poet for one, really loved him and said so. Literary ladies, infatuate as only such can be, followed him, wrote him, composed gushing sonnets to him. Of course, one always wonders if the real man was at all involved in such antics, or if it was only the ladies' projection of their fantasies of romantic liaison. Robinson had his own fantasies, and perhaps the late long poems show something of their nature in the quality of the names of his heroines and female temptresses: Laramie, Natalie, Gabrielle, Karen, Althea . . .

The last years really found him retreating more and more from the society which had finally made a place for him. Lilla Perry the painter, who did a striking portrait of Robinson, gave him the loan of her studio on Beacon Hill in Boston, but he did no work there; he recovered from the arduous labor of the months at the MacDowell Colony and mulled over memories, ideas, the notions that might come to be poems, while he smoked Sweet Caporals incessantly and consumed detective stories. But he kept up his correspondence with many old friends, including Mrs. Richards. The letters show he had lost none of his awareness, wit and singleness of purpose. He had grown tired. The long poems which seem to us so perfunctory exhausted him, yet the most exhausting and the finest, *Amaranth,* comes very late. He felt sure, and in his diffident way said so, that this time he had made the poem he wanted to make: "I don't think of anything just like it," he wrote to Hagedorn, "and I don't think it is altogether bad." It wasn't. He had come back strongly, but the vitality had gone and by this time the cancer that would kill him must have been in part responsible for the weariness, though the long years we have read about could do it readily without help. As he observed in a letter to Lewis Isaacs, his friend from Peterborough and financial adviser, "Going dry doesn't settle everything." It did not. He wrote that when he was already deep in *Amaranth,* and he knew that though he had gone through a period of dryness and compulsive production, the well still held good water. That may explain his deathbed anxiety over the proofs of *King Jasper.* Sick and dying though he was, he knew he still had something to say.

The long drought that had set in by the time *The Man Who Died Twice* was published had ended. The long poem he had always meant to write—a poem of memory, experience, dream and acceptance—could not get itself written until he had got rid of the motif of the triangle and the Meredithian arid glibness. In a letter to Mrs. Richards written roughly a year after he had finished *Amaranth,* he says this: "I don't hear Meredith mentioned nowadays, but Henry James is still going strong in his always limited way. Meredith was too much a novelist to be a poet and too much a poet to be a novelist and too much a verbal snob to be either. And still he was a genius . . . I have always smelt a disagreeable personality leaking its way out through Meredith's pages. I don't believe he had any feelings—except for himself." And perhaps that saved Robinson from going along with the Meredithian propensity that had so grown upon him: that capacity to feel with and for others. He can understand King Mark and his not-so-simple attitude towards the lovers whose death he has occasioned, as he can feel for the curiously frustrated and incommunicable souls who make up the dramatis personae of the long poem which is all the long poems from 1923 to 1933. If we can see the hand of Meredith in the rhetoric and dialogue of many of these, we can see some of the honest intensity of *Modern Love* in parts of *Merlin* and in the final soliloquy of Mark in *Tristram.* Yet, James rather than Meredith was "his true Penelope," that hallucinated, memory-haunted and emblematic James of the later stories and novellas. His "always limited way" resembled Robinson's; both buried deep in themselves the "notes of a son and brother" which they would later remember and turn to. If James went to Europe for his complex patterns, Robinson found something similar in that combination world of Gardiner, New York and cosmopolis. Both men were inward. They did their reading and their learning early. Each knew physical and psychic wounds from an early age. Robinson's poetry always kept a prose in view, as James's prose had always sought the figurative, echoic and rhetorical resourcefulness of poetry. One would not want to push the parallel too far, yet *Amaranth* has its striking affinities with James's stories of artists and writers, with pieces like "The Jolly Corner," as certain Robinson poems, longer and shorter, remind of "The Beast in the Jungle" and perhaps even *The Ambassadors;* consider *Matthias at the Door,* for example, among the long poems, and "Mortmain," "The Woman and The Wife" and a great many other poems which deal with honesty and openness in love and all human relationships.

King Jasper is another matter. By no means as successful a poem as *Amaranth,* it still shows change and advance of a kind. Robinson did not go back, return to the triangles and the nitpicking psychologizing of the ten years' between 1923 and 1933. For one thing, immediately after he finished *Amaranth* in the fall of 1933, he fell really ill, ill in body and soul. He had worked himself to the very edge, and all the malaise he had felt for the past couple of years seemed to reach a peak. He began to have bad headaches, which were not helped by a curious accident he suffered walking a Boston street. Some boys were playing baseball in a vacant lot and a ball struck him on the head. The old ear trouble flared up, and though X-ray showed no infection or break, he himself felt near the breaking point. Providentially he had recently got to know Merrill Moore, the distinguished psychiatrist and poet, one of the Fugitive group who for a time had made Vanderbilt University the center of American poetry. Moore had become a kind of soul-doctor for many writers and "life's delicate children," as Mann put it. There can be no doubt that he helped his new friend and patient, helped him to return to New York and face the world of men and women he had known but had recently retreated from. By the spring he felt really revived and went eagerly back to Peterborough to begin *King Jasper.* According to Hagedorn, Merrill Moore was able to get Robinson to face and to accept his long-suppressed resentment of his father. I do not *know* it, but I think that Robinson had long since exorcised the evil spirit of resentment against his mother by means of certain poems, not the least of which was "For a Dead Lady." And it may well be, though God knows it may just as well not be, that King Jasper himself is Edward Robinson and the poet a composite of his son Jasper, and Zoe's lover, the hating and loving, fiery radical Hebron. Esther Bates, the devoted amanuensis and disciple who seems to have lived her life in him and his poetry, asked him about the allegory, and he observed that "Zoe is knowledge and the child of King Jasper, who is ignorance. Without ignorance there can be no knowledge." It is possible that Merrill Moore managed to reconcile Robinson to his memories of his father by de-emphasizing Edward's "ignorance" of his son's nature and need and stressing his role in making that son into a poet. One might go on and on with a personal Freudian or pop-Freudian symbolic analysis of *King Jasper* at the expense of the allegory Robinson clearly intended. Yet I do feel that Merrill Moore and *Amaranth* combined to release certain resources of poetic power that had long been confined. But Robinson was a dying man.

He came back to Boston from his last summer in Peterborough and stayed awhile with Burnham and another old friend, Edward Carty Ranck, to whom he had dedicated *Nicodemus*. Both men were devoted to him, and both belonged to that group of failures and outsiders with which he had identified himself from youth: Pope, Betts, French, Burnham, Ranck and others. All men who had suffered greatly, known poverty and rejection, in some cases madness. Of them all Burnham and Ranck were closest to him, and perhaps, as Hagedorn suggests, it was of them along with himself that he dreamed recurrently, of three men who have fallen into a deep well and can be drawn out on the thinnest of threads if they will only believe. Yet before they can reach safety, one doubts and they drop, to sink under the water. Absurd. But the dream was one that Merrill Moore coped with. Robinson was too old and too set in his nature to change loyalties. Did he feel that these men dragged him down? French had in effect threatened his life. Did some of the other friends threaten his soul's life? Whatever the explanation, Robinson made himself responsible for Burnham and Ranck, as he had for Pope. When he left them to go back to New York, he seemed to have the mark of death on him. By January the doctors in New York Hospital had cut him open and closed him up again. There was nothing more they could do.

Meanwhile, the critics had not been idle. He might as well have had no success at all, since the tide had turned against him at the end as it had from the beginning. *Amaranth* got rough handling from the professional reviewers and critics. The more Philistine publications were respectful, but the younger people and journals like *The New Republic* simply condescended and treated the poem as proof of senility. In a sense, the long poems had done him disservice, and the newer generation did not bother to look for something new in an old poet. He had once complained of an earlier generation, "Why don't they read me?" He might have said it all again for a new time and a new crop. They did not bother. The earlier era had its poetasters. The later had its own brand. But the hardest word of all, in a way, he did not live to hear. *King Jasper* came out in 1936 with a foreword by Robert Frost. Again, not only is the record clear, in Frost's own letters, but the foreword itself is damning enough with the faintest and most condescending of praise. But it scarcely mattered: Robinson's work had gone out of fashion before it was "in" with the "in" crowd, and to this day such representation as his work finds in anthologies derives from other anthologies. They did not—they do not—read him.

X

The Poet as Modernist

Writers are rarely fortunate in their critics over the long haul. Broadly speaking, two kinds of critics do the most damage: the total professional and the poetry lover. When one is tempered by the other, a poet can get someone very good indeed, but nowadays poetry lovers hardly exist (not under sixty years of age, anyhow), and the real harm comes from the pros, who are either of the exacerbated-academic or the New York–British school. They do not like poetry, particularly the poetry they write about, unless it is by a certain few friends and potentates. Party lines shift and favorites rise and fall dizzily: one has to be there constantly making the scene. The truly "in" poet is not so much a poet as an industry. Where would thousands be without Wallace Stevens? The sociologist who developed a study of the poet as a creator of employment and contributor to the gross national product might just earn for himself a professorship and foundation grants for life, thereby making the circle of symbiosis or parasitism at once complete and efficient. Nevertheless, even the most cynically opportunist criticism has value when it points towards the work and says however partially, Read It. In effect, what more can or should a critic do, for his living and every reader's else? The critic, if that's what he is, who here speaks to the reader aims to give that reader no more, and he hopes no less, than a version of his own reading of a poet so that the reader, in disgust, enthusiasm or inertia will be carried to the main source and read the poetry. Go thou and do likewise.

I have myself gone through many stages in my reading of Robinson's poetry, a reading which first began in 1936. There was a time—I would guess some fifteen years—when I read him not at all and gave no thought to the work that had once so fascinated me. Coming back to it after all that time, I found that many of the poems I had ignored now spoke to me most powerfully, and many of those I had admired seemed to wear less well. I am sure such is the case with any poet's work under comparable circumstances. What I should like to stress here, though, is that what Robinson said of the work of Crabbe in his sonnet on that subject holds true in this case: "There yet remains what fashion cannot kill," and even more than that, "we can feel . . . the vigor of his name . . ." Anyone who has really read Robinson's poems must find them at last as parts of his own sensibility, a rebuke for false feeling and cheap technique, a good bracing word for honesty and a stoic facing of reality. I do not propose in this chapter to attempt anything as absurd as a Ranking of Poets. I would like only to reinforce certain points made at the beginning of this book, and to do so I think we might need to look at a few matters commonly dealt with at length in any reasonably comprehensive study of a reasonably comprehensive poet.

Two books seem to me indispensable for an understanding of Robinson's debt to the literature of the past, and to his place in the climate of ideas of his time, which is in part our own. The first by Edwin Fussell and the second by W. R. Robinson I have listed in the Bibliography. They strike me as not only the best in their particular purviews but also as the finest studies of Robinson's work from any point of view, always with the addition of Yvor Winters' critique. Yet they proceed upon the assumption that not only have most readers of poetry read a lot of Robinson, but that what they have read is the best, or that the best is included along with the less good. It is a truism that one should not look for certain subjects, qualities and themes in a writer who has not the slightest intention of providing such. Equally, a poet cannot expect to attract readers who dislike that poet's poetic nature. And above all else, any poet good or bad has to hope for a reader who can stand a certain amount of salutary boredom to give the poet time to make his effects:

it takes time and it takes motion and in that interval a reader may escape. A number of readers have never approached Robinson except by way of the bromidic anthology pieces or else by way of his Ideas and Philosophy. Yet what for a time killed interest in Robinson is today killing Eliot and will very soon get around to doing in Wallace Stevens. What the average critic cannot get through his head is the fact that if it's ideas you want, go elsewhere than to poetry. Stevens criticism today is full of paraphrases of his thought—about aesthetics, art, the imagination, reality, modernism, this world and the next, if any. Eliot criticism, which used to be mere explication de texte and a tracing of allusions, has now gone into the theological and philosophical phases. And most of those today who read Eliot do so in spite of these things. So with Robinson. What most of his original protagonists said about him may or may not have been true, for them and for us; but for us today it is largely irrelevant, concerned as it is with a psychology and an ontology— indeed a whole view of reality—which we cannot share. That does not mean that they understand him less well but only that his work, like that of any fine poet, has both variety and depth, and many readers can find many different sorts of things depending on where they look and from which angle.

Earlier I remarked that Robinson was a city poet, perhaps our first and finest. We can see easily enough how little natural detail or physical detail of any kind there is in the poetry, and by city poet we do not have to mean someone who runs on about neon, air hammers and subways. One or two references in Hart Crane's poetry can lead to intemperate comment on how he integrated the machine into poetic sensibility, which is perfect nonsense. No one has yet, and there is no pressing reason why anyone should. What Robinson does is to take New York and lower Manhattan particularly as a mise en scène, the locale where his plots happen. "The White Lights," "Calverley's," "Old Trails" above all evoke by a kind of subtle effluence, and by place names too, the flavor of Bohemian Manhattan, of Robinson's Village and lower Broadway. "The Poor Relation" rather remarkably deals not with an old spinster in the manner and locality of a Jewett story, but with a nameless woman in the anonymity of an apartment in the Bronx or Queens. Many

of the more "plotted" sonnets strongly suggest an urban setting
—"Doctor of Billiards" evokes the pool halls of Robinson's city
evenings, as "Alma Mater" must surely relate one of the occasions when the egregious French burst in on him in one of his
dingy rooms. These poems take place in a world of men and
frequently a world of streets, with a sense of crowds and urban
noise and dirt in the background. Has any other poet ever
used the name Yonkers in a poem? The very prosaicness of
the name adds irony to that masterpiece of irony, "Old Trails."
Above all, where else could Robinson place his fierce old ranting
philosopher of "The Wandering Jew" but in the Manhattan
he knew in his New York days—or more especially nights?
These poems are poems of late at night, in bleak streets and
cheap taverns and poor rooms. No one, I would venture to
guess, gets more of the true grimness of the "vue de la vie de
bohème" than he does: poverty, sickness, human wastage, loneliness and despair. He writes of these things and he can make us
feel what he himself knew, through others and in his own soul
and body. Did he not tell Isaacs, when the latter chided him
for giving money away to bums and panhandlers and chronically
indigent acquaintances, "You've never walked the streets of
New York without a nickel in your pocket"? Poverty never yet
made a poet, and it has unmade many. It can be said that af-
fluence "concentrates the mind wonderfully"; Robinson knew
that higher things and the muse were all very well, but a drink
and a meal did better on a cold night.

His use of the urban scene, like his use of the rural, depends
on the appropriateness to that scene of character, event and
memory. I tend to think that certain poems commonly ascribed
to a Tilbury Town provenience actually belong to New York;
they have that feel. Yet wherever we are in the poems, we are
never far from a dwelling, a town and a number of people,
people who often constitute the "we" of such poems as "Eros
Turannos." How often the poems convey a sense of the pressure
of the public world upon the private, of the outside trying to
break in. The private self tries to hide its grief from the world
which in its turn insists on getting at, if not the truth of the
private matter, the heart's blood of the private self. "Home,"
as Robinson puts it in "Eros Turannos," "becomes a place where

she can hide," and her attempt to hide her feelings and her condition simply provokes the world to more and wilder speculation:
"As if the story of a house / Were told or ever could be." Robinson sees the life of man or woman as an interplay between
inside and outside; unlike most modern poets he does not assume
that the former is true and the latter false. He assumes, along
with Conrad, that illusion may indeed save or at any rate
preserve, as the illusion of the mother in "The Gift of God" and
of Oakes in "Two Gardens in Linndale" take on a character almost sacramental. Yet the illusion of the protagonist of "The
Wandering Jew," while it keeps him from the destructive reality of his self-deception, has no saving quality about it. The
man may be pathetic, but he uses all his resources of intellect
and learning to deny, like Mephistopheles. The poor relation
in her closed room, the aging prostitutes of "Veteran Sirens,"
the protagonist of "Old Trails," Eben Flood, John Evereldown
and many more are locked away from reality and their fellows,
and Robinson finds all sorts of fascinating variations on the
theme of this isolation. And we also see that if the individuals
so isolated suffer certain consequences, so we who have the
temerity to judge them do so at our peril, for which among us
knows the true "story of a house"?

Robinson's poetry never aims at myth-making, a symbolic and
self-contained world of aesthetic or metaphysical truth. He does
not, like Pound, write a personal and artistic diary, nor like
Eliot a biography of modern man in his pilgrimage from atrophy
through agony to rebirth, nor does he attempt the creation of a
world of the imagination like Stevens. He tries to see what is set
before him. In "Hillcrest" he sets the bounds to human ambition
and what a man may achieve; contemplation of one's own am-
bitions and achievements can have the salutary effect of making
one see how little it amounts to and how much of vanity and
self-delusion there is in what a man calls his life. These are
hard precepts and of course they express but one side of Robinson's poetic creed, but significantly, what this view of man and
his world suggests is that art is about man and his world, that
it is about how to see things as a stoic sees them. The civilized
man aims at wisdom. In "Hillcrest" Robinson shows that the
wisdom he usually finds after contemplation comes down to the

realization that his life and work are "unfound" and full of "error." Yet a man must go on from there.

In many of the long poems, that is what the Robinsonian hero, to use an inappropriate epithet, attempts to do after he has come to a certain self-knowledge. Of course, as in "The Man Against the Sky," he may chose suicide—indeed, if he is a materialist he can properly do nothing else—but in *Lancelot* the hero rides out and away from Guenevere and Arthur and all the betrayal, error and self-deception that the realm and its great folk have come to. He leaves the Queen to her cloistered penitence while he goes out to seek and to find the "Light." Fargo, in *Amaranth,* on the verge of re-establishing his great illusion of art, dreams his vision and utterly rejects at last such lies in favor of the naked truth. The expense of spirit involved we must imagine; that expense may in fact be what redeems a man and makes him man indeed. Stoicism, in the Robinsonian view, has more than negative virtue, because the power to see the truth, tell it to oneself if no one else, and to act upon it partakes of the heroic and is what makes civilization and keeps it.

In all of this we remember that many or most of the poems are about people. Not the historical characters of Browning nor the hieratic emblems of Tennyson nor the lay figures of Eliot, but real people in such ordinarily trying circumstances as poverty, loneliness, abandonment, failure, sickness, exhaustion, despair. The problems have no particular modernity or modernism about them; some in fact, like the situation of the woman in "Eros Turannos," might seem old-fashioned. Why doesn't she just divorce him—go to Las Vegas or Mexico, and as they say, live a little? But even today, does everyone really do such things? And Robinson in all his poems insists on the uniqueness of the man or woman and the event. The stories are exemplary only as we can find the general in the particular. The poet never tells us to extend the meaning; in fact, he warns us against doing so. That qualifying tendency which so complicates the movement of the longer poems in the shorter often makes for increased complexity and suggestion. Robinson deals in plot, situation, action as most poets who write about specific dilemmas deal with scene, juxtaposition of temperaments, internal rumination, as in "The Lovesong of J. Alfred Prufrock." The personae of Pound are cultural phenomena, not people, and the Crispins or whoever of Stevens manifest certain aesthetic ideas of the poet or become ironic observers, aesthetic speculators, "comedians."

I have been using Pound, Eliot and Stevens in contrast with Robinson for the reason that these poets succeed him in the line of modernism. All three overshadow American poetry of the period 1914–1945 and the tone and example they set, though no longer all-prevailing, constituted, for most readers, critics and academicians that marriage of the new with the traditional which they knew as modernity in poetry. These three men compose the standard version of what American poetry of the twentieth century has been. One must qualify of course: Crane, W. C. Williams and some others have their professors and had their influence, and Frost stands outside the battle, alone on his cracker barrel. Or so seems to run the Revised Standard Version. Certainly the names I have just mentioned must be given precedence as the most widely influential American poets of the time. With them American poetry became sophisticated, cultured, cosmopolitan and sure of itself. Thoroughly convinced of its regenerative powers, it swept "English" poetry aside, and today no English poet of any consequence whatever can keep from going to school to the Americans.

Robinson has had nothing like such influence, in his time or since. Yet his own voice is unmistakable; a Robinson poem, good or bad, speaks to us in accents and a tone we recognize at once. With some poets such tones derive from originality, eccentricity, an attempt to seize rather than gain attention: Hopkins, Blake, Donne. Hence they attract imitators, and something of the sort seems to be, or have been, the case with the poets I have just mentioned. But writers of a middle style, the humanist, civilized and ratiocinative minds and imaginations, aim at a continuity of tradition, mode or sensibility, rather than a rupture or divagation. The Robinsons of literature build on a tradition in which they have been nurtured and which they simply manipulate closer to their hearts' desire. There is nothing spectacular or original in Wordsworth; his power resides in his great technical command of traditional forms wedded to a personal vision and voice of unquestionable authenticity. Which is to say that he is never phony, as Robinson is never phony. Even when they delude themselves and fall into a boring mumble, we sense an honest man feeling around in the dark for something to say and to mean. For in the last analysis, the poet of the middle style, in order to remain faithful to his vision of ordinary men in a recognizably real world, must risk the pedestrian and the banal, just as the poet of originality, in order to fly ever higher, risks the catastrophic fall and disintegration. Our time has favored the latter type, obviously; what Wordsworth meant by his statement in the Preface to the second edition of *Lyrical Ballads* to the effect that greater and greater emphasis on originality would mean larger and larger doses of "gross stimulants" has proved true indeed. Originality, once suspect in art, has become synonymous with art itself. What the word means in poetry is a vexed question. To the reader of Robinson's poetry the word means something wholly different.

Pound, Stevens and Eliot sought another kind of tradition, a ransacking of foreign capitals to bring back to the provinces great culture, grand culture. Pound in the *Pisan Cantos* claims that he had "gathered from the air a live tradition," cosmopolitan, eclectic, arcane. Stevens, in his remark that French and English are really the same language, certainly shows that he wants to break out into a new speech of his own, which in effect he does, to remake language and sensibility in order to change "things as they are" into the abstractions of the imagination. His foreign capitals are the tropics of his fancy. Eliot's are the masterworks of past masters and present symbolists, literary capitals derived from literature.

Robinson's foreign country is the country of the human heart and mind in Gardiner, Maine, and in New York. A far more parochial sort than his great successors, he worked entirely with the given, with what he had known and read and felt up to the time he was, let us say, in his middle twenties; everything after that simply refines a technique and response and adds complexity to material the mind and imagination and memory had assimilated. Subjects may reflect new experience; the poetry gains enormously in its capacity to modulate and to express, but essentially Robinson does not change between first and last. Like Wordsworth, he has been accused of going steadily downhill as his career wore on, and as is the case with Wordsworth, the accusation turns out to hold good only in part and only if we ignore subtleties while holding out for "gross stimulants." But a man can get as drunk on champagne as canned heat. Whether either is good for what ails him may be a real question. Certainly, though, champagne won't kill him—not for a long time, anyhow. What a reader of poetry of all kinds and schools should know is: all a poet needs is genius, and a little luck.

Yet when we have said all that, what about the individual poem and how it goes about being a poem, the poem it is in itself? I take it that any poem that works was once a modern poem. Nothing can work in the future that does not work in the present. Poems are made, they do not grow. If you make a poem and it does not work, leaving it alone to cure itself as though it were a greensick youth cannot help, because a poem that does not work is a defective mechanism which neglect cannot mend. Poems which, ignored in youth, turn out to be great, have not and never had defects—only defective readers or readings. A reading of a Robinson poem today as compared, let us say, with one in 1914, suggests differences of civilization and temper with which this study has nothing to do. What I would like to attempt now, however, is a kind of full-scale analysis of one or two of the major short poems, with the purpose of providing something for contemporary readers to fight back against, if nothing else. And in this regard let me say that I propose a kind of reading which commits all the heresies, ancient and modern, which I can think of offhand, from that of paraphrase to all kinds of interpretations that whoever may be chic this week must excoriate. Housman kept himself from thinking of lines of poetry while shaving because his skin would crawl and he would cut himself. Emily Dickinson felt as though the top of her head were coming off when she thought of certain passages. No man or woman who has not and does not feel this way about poems from time to time will have any luck with poetry ever. And of course a kind of goose-pimple or topless school of criticism will never make a Ph.D., however wild the scene may be. There are times when, for one's own sake as a reader and for the sake of the poem itself, a long and steady look at the poem's parts can give a renewed awareness of the miraculous whole. No critic should rejoice in either his cleverness or the poem's infinite resource and sagacity. It got there, if it did, "by the stairway of surprise." Lucky, ingenious, shrewd critic to spot the route it took!

Robinson's poems, when they work, speak out loud. We should read them aloud; they are meant to be heard. Unlike the sort of poet who cultivates an idiosyncratic manner of speech by means of which he projects his poem, Robinson seems to have had in mind a flexible, masculine speaker, one who witholds judgment, sees as far as the facts warrant, and can command varied effects within a modest but not narrow range. A comfortable, easy-seeming man, this speaker. He will tell us some things that we do not want to know, but we get stuck with them because before we knew what was happening, that insinuating, modest voice had got in and was halfway up the stairway of surprise. Such is the case with "Old Trails."

The speaker, if we know our Robinson, is someone we have met before: disenchanted, cagey, reticent. He has been through the mill and has known too many failures and successes, too much bad luck and good management, to be very surprised at anything that happens. His interlocutor we have also met before, in one of his many Robinsonian guises, as Captain Craig, for example. But in this case as in all the others which have true poetic quality, something different happens. In the first place we must imagine the milieu so effortlessly and quickly sketched for us. Washington Square, MacDougal Street no doubt, a basement bar and later a dingy room in a boarding house— Robinson's own Village bohemia. One of the drifting writers, intellectuals, hangers-on of all the arts and philosophies has come back to his old haunts after ten years of drifting. Here is one of Robinson's own friends, a man like Burnham, perhaps, or Mowry Saben, or even always and forever, Robinson himself. But he is also a work of fiction, the quintessential American, artist-bohemian variety, vintage 1910, let us say. He has roamed the world for ten years looking for—what? Himself? Success? Both. And at last, in order that he may find that new and of course true self which shall succeed, he must go back to the place he started from, amid the ghosts of all the failures including his own. He must face them all down—in effect, he must do them down, kill the ghost inside himself and the ghosts of his old friends who haunt him with their failure, in order to live again, to cast off the old and to become that new man who after five years, "sauntered into fame." The poem is of course about failure and success, but more particularly, about the cost of each and both. As the protagonist says, "I haven't failed; I've merely not achieved." In order to reach the point at which achievement can begin, he has to come all the way back along the "old trails" to his old haunts and his old friends, now mostly mere "ghosts," there to face his own "ghost." When he and his companion, the narrator, finally leave the "old room on Eleventh Street," he has become a new man. They go from "the newest of hotels" to the Metropolitan Opera to see *Boris Godunov,* and the protagonist, in exaltation, sees something of his own career in that of Boris, though Robinson leaves out any corroborative detail, and sings to himself that "God lives . . . and I'm the man." The rest is commentary by the narrator. The protagonist has his five years of toil in the wilderness of Yonkers and then achieves the success he predicted for himself. At the end of the poem the narrator reflects that perhaps, despite the triumph over prediction and odds, such a triumph has another side and that an ambiguous one. It is not that Robinson simply sounds the Browning note of the "failure of success"; more than that, Robinson dramatizes the slightly shady character of the man and his "fame." What did he do, after all? He has won the "adulations of applauding hosts" which suggests the celebrity rather than the man of true fame, the timeserver who, as it seems, betrays his past and the ghosts of his former friends, choosing "a safer way / Than growing old alone among the ghosts."

The climax of the poem comes during the performance of *Boris,* that savage story of guilt, remorse, hallucination and violence. One need not push matters at all far to see how much Robinson implies by "the bells in *Boris."* The protagonist of the poem, like Boris, has betrayed and murdered the past and may have paid too great a price for fame and applause. The bells which call the monks to prayer also call on the people of Russia to revolt against Boris. As the man in Robinson's poem sits at the Metropolitan watching the tumult of the great opera,

he exclaims "I'm the man," as Boris might have when he murdered Dmitri to gain the throne. And the poem concludes with
the narrator's "I wish the bells in *Boris* would be quiet."

The plot is an interesting variation on a familiar theme, one
that we find adumbrated in as early a poem as "Supremacy,"
written when he was in college, and explored to its fullest in
the next to last of his published poems, *Amaranth.* "Old Trails"
tells of a man who, like Fargo, has gone to New York to "be
an artist"—whatever that may mean. Gradually he begins to
find out that he may not have the magic, that unlike Fernando
Nash of *The Man Who Died Twice* he had never "had it—once,"
had in fact, like Fargo, never had it at all. He disappears and
simply keeps moving until, ten years later, he returns to the
scene of the crime, exactly as Fargo does. It is at this point that
the poem actually begins, though any reading of Robinson will
provide enough material for us to fill the gap. In the narrator's
words, "memory meets the unfulfilled" and back to Eleventh
Street comes the Robinsonian failure with all his "ghosts" waiting for him. But the additional turn of the screw in this case,
the supreme irony, comes when having faced his ghosts and
taken only a few things from his old room, he refuses to face
the fact of his lack of artistic power; "hope lives on clamorous,"
though he freely admits he does not know what he hopes for.
But we know, or soon shall, for doesn't he add, "Broadway's
hard-throated siren-calls"? He wants fame and he knows or
thinks he knows that he will find it; the performance of *Boris*
he takes for a sign: "God lives . . . and I'm the man." All those,
like the narrator, who had predicted for him an accelerating
decline into despair and suicide, like the ruins in *Amaranth,*
find their perhaps willful prophecy countermanded by his sudden emergence from Yonkers into fame; Robinson implies that
our man has become a successful playwright, and with his own
experience in that attempt fresh in his mind ("Old Trails"
comes from that period), Robinson also implies that success on
Broadway means commercial success which very probably has
nothing to do with artistic merit. Still, honest man that he is,
the narrator sees how neatly his old friend has triumphed over
them all and they "would shrivel to deny it." Nonetheless, he
has to feel that somewhere something went wrong. The famous

playwright has succeeded and scored off all his old friends who predicted for him ruin. They were half right: didn't he call himself a "ruin who meant well"? Something in the narrator wants to applaud him, like the world at large; something else wants to condemn him for cowardice, betrayal. He has chosen "a safer way" of using his talent. For Robinson, the only right way for the artist is to stay with one's ghosts and memories. Out of the "old echoes" comes the true poetry.

If this discussion of "Old Trails" seems too dependent on what I have called "plot," perhaps that alone may show why I consider Robinson a poet with a prose in view and one who needs to be understood and read in ways quite foreign to those usually employed for the reading and understanding of late Romantic and modern poets. We have got used to minimizing action, physical and moral, and to exaggerating ironic, symbolic and imagistic patterns. Robinson's poetry can sustain such analyses as used to be common in criticism; indeed, "Old Trails" has all kinds of imagistic and verbal motifs which could be exhaustively traced. The point is, simply, that in Robinson's poems such things seem to the unpracticed eye absent because they serve a purpose rather than assume that purpose. They are there to make the whole poem go and to serve a "plot," an action: the moral destiny of a person or persons. In "Old Trails" there are three moral entities to consider: the protagonist, the narrator, and that *tertium aliquid,* the poet or the "hypocrite lecteur," who prowls around the edges of the action and overhears and ponders and judges, or perhaps fails to decide. The strategy is a constant in the successful short poems of the plotted variety and it represents one of Robinson's major inventions. The poets with whom he is, or was, commonly lumped, like Masters and Lindsay, for all they wrote about people, had no conception of anything remotely like this. Nor did Browning, whose "barbarism" as Santayana calls it, or relativism as Langbaum has it, makes of his people either strongly flavored representative types or moral chameleons. They fascinate, but it is the total immersion in their element that provides the fascination. Browning is a poet of surfaces—and brilliant surfaces they are. Robinson goes deeper, but the surface is always there. "Between the gray Arch and the old Hotel."

"Old Trails" we can call a reflective narrative, perhaps; it would be difficult to call it a lyric. The stanza form, rhyming quatrains in pentameter, is of the commonest kind. Hardly a word or syntactical construction deviates from the ordinary middle style. What keeps the thing from becoming a bore? In the first place it gets going at once without flourishes but wholly efficiently. Robinson's usual tactic is to begin with a flat state-ment of physical or emotional action: "Eros Turannos" begins with "She fears him"; here, it is "I met him," as in "The Mill" it is "The Miller's wife had waited long," and in "Mr. Flood's Party," it is "Old Eben Flood climbing alone one night." Some of the poems, notably the tricky ones, start off with a burst that seems melodramatic, too calculatedly arresting and hence self-defeating. Two examples might be the opening lines of "The Clinging Vine" and in a quieter way, "Lisette and Eileen" which unfailingly makes me think of "When you and I were young, Maggie," surely a classic case of "mnemonic irrelevancy." The strategy of seizing the attention in this mode, that of the reflective narrative, has to be carefully planned and yet seem casual, offhand. "Because he was a butcher . . ." has a kind of throwaway air about it which immediately catches us up by its seeming inappropriateness. The poem is a sonnet and Robin-son, after his earliest experiments in the form, tried to revivify it by giving it a new kind of content. Perhaps Meredith's *Modern Love* had an influence, but more likely what Robinson did with the form belongs with the rest of his original contributions: he extended the range of what poetry can talk about, and he settled a new country of discourse, one which squatters would overrun but which his own private preserve will outlast.

But there are other sorts of shorter poem and one in par-ticular which I might here classify as the plotless reflective lyric. Having obvious affinities with poems like "Old Trails," it yet deals more generally with moral and emotional states. At times Robinson will make such a poem both more particular as to character and more lyrical as to technique and feeling, as in let us say, "Luke Havergal" or "For a Dead Lady"; at other times, the situation is less particular, more abstractly described and rises only at climactic moments to lyric intensity, as in "The Gift of God" and "Mr. Flood's Party." In many or most of all these, irony determines the detached and sometimes pitying tone, yet the irony has nothing in common with that of the neo-Metaphysical school which became fashionable late in Robinson's lifetime, the school of the Donne revival, of Eliot, Ransom, Tate and others. In their case irony is a poetic rather than a human response, a poetic strategy, a means of distancing and a way of dealing more objectively, as they thought, with Romantic ideas. True to its own era, it expresses a nostalgia, longing, frustrated desire and a sense of lostness far more effective than anything Thomas Wolfe's fulminations can contrive. The jaded, world-weary and wholly knowing pose so common in the 1920s with novelists like Michael Arlen and James Branch Cabell assumes in the poets I mention something more serious and relevant to the time. Ransom can still move us because his ironic pose becomes second nature, a true way of dealing with experience. He shows us how to believe and to be sceptical at the same time, as Eliot in the *Four Quartets* shows us how to set about getting ourselves reborn. But in the cases of all these poets, it seems to me, the ironic style is not the man but the poet. We seldom if ever have a sense of a particular man and his sensibility talking to us. Indeed, these poems and poets often are very nearly "anonymous" in Ransom's sense of the word.

How different is Robinson's case, and how far from his that of most contemporary poetry. Today much that we read aims at a language and an imagery which, wholly unremarkable in themselves, shall evoke another language and another imagery not written out in the text but which will, so to speak, leak through after we ponder the poem awhile. So at any rate I interpret the whole strategy of such poets as Denise Levertov, Robert Creeley, Charles Olson—all the Black Mountain and W. C. Williams schools. Robinson as always takes the middle way. To him poetic language is neither public nor private speech, neither subterranean mumble nor the music of the spheres, but a combination of all of these. With something added—and the something I might describe as Subject and Approach.

Choice of subject and one's particular angle of vision upon that subject give rise to the characteristic Robinsonian irony. That irony may or may not express itself in the language itself, in the incidentals, but it must find outlets in some kind of stated or implied comparison of the way things look with the way they really are. The Robinsonian tactic which he can use to great effect is to suggest all sorts of alternatives without ever coming down in favor of one in particular, of offering a solution. The point here is not that he is neutral but that he finds too much in any human dilemma to pretend to more than suggestion—"as if the story of a house / Were told or ever could be." That characterizes the mode, the tone of voice, the whole attitude towards human weakness. When he writes well in this mode, Robinson never becomes merely presentational, does not simply give us the problem and abandon it, say to us, here it is, *you* figure it out. He turns it this way and that, then puts it to us: Are you God? No, and neither is the poet. We do not here have a case of moral relativism, as Langbaum describes it; rather I think Robinson tells us to go ahead and judge if we feel we must, but be sure of two things first: that you understand and that you accept your own verdict as applicable to your own case.

I have chosen "Hillcrest" as a poem which exemplifies the latter mode of which I have been speaking. Subject and approach to it not only must have come first to Robinson's mind when he imagined the poem, but the very abstract, ruminating manner of dealing with the subject, the at once detached yet concerned attitude towards a state of mind both personal and general indicates the methods, or one method, he uses to deal with that kind of gray area in one's being which is both public and private, wholly individual yet common to all men of sensibility. The poem, dedicated to Mrs. MacDowell, he wrote at the Colony, and the outward scene, such as it is, probably suggests the view from his cabin towards Monadnock. The theme of the poem is quintessential Robinson, and it sums up, as it unwinds through the verse, that view of life which he came at early and which he never abandoned. Call it transcendentalism, his "philosophy" —what you will: he himself said that it was "mostly a statement of my inability to accept a mechanistic interpretation of the universe and life." It might be a constructive exercise to bear in mind "The Man Against the Sky" when reading "Hillcrest" if only to observe how much more successfully Robinson deals in the latter poem with his "inability." It occurs in the volume that bears the title of the former poem and shows the extremes of Robinson's technique: one is rhetorical, a virtuoso set piece in the grand manner; the other is simple, in the familiar middle style, and conveying the sense of a man speaking to men. No eminently quotable lines, no elaborate and managed metaphors; the poem speaks quietly and with assurance.

As we know, many critics, at the time of the first publication of "The Man Against the Sky" and since then as well, attacked Robinson for his hesitancy, his seeming inability ever to take a side in the poem, to say what it is he believes. Perhaps they have a valid point, if in fact that must be the poet's avowed and necessary purpose and duty. It need not be. The poem works out in detail the alternatives, as the poet sees them, to his own position of "transcendentalism" or the "Inability to accept a mechanistic interpretation of life." He shows in a sometimes eloquent style the twistings and turnings by means of which his "man" may achieve a certain intellectual and spiritual position or state, and the poem concludes with the Robinsonian descent in darkness to a tidal water.

Some of the key words in "The Man Against the Sky" are "humility," "wisdom" and "vision." In "Hillcrest" such words and abstractions become the themes and subjects, the texture itself, of the poem. What the former recites in detail, the latter implies, touches on delicately, and leaves. The former is loaded with abstract nouns and with ornate comparisons not always of the happiest kind, but "Hillcrest" starts with what is here at hand, the scene in front of us, and in those firm and yet hesitant rhythms we know so well, talks of the Great Universals without ever naming them. The poem then offers one of the great Robinsonian performances in the anti-Romantic treatment of a Romantic theme. If anyone wants to call it Robinson's epistemological masterpiece, perhaps that would suit, provided we all know what the functional term means. What Robinson means in the poem comes clear: whatever it is you think you have learned from "life," you probably have not. It all consists, to go back to Mann's phrase, in "getting used to not getting used." Now notions as comfortless as this do not set well with readers—or even with critics who are likely to want their bleakness more flamboyant, *ängstlich* and foreign, as though no Yankee has a right to discuss such things without a license from Kafka or Rilke, writers of whom Robinson may never have heard. But a doctorate in comparative literature does not, fortunately, make a poet, and if Robinson had only slight acquaintance with the literature of the subject, he at least had two advantages: he was a poet and he had been through the experience. One might also add that he had the courage to face that experience in his poetry.

"Hillcrest" looks directly at what elsewhere Robinson calls the "vision" or the "Orient word" or the "Light." The operative word here is "see" as in so many other poems, but in this instance the poem starts with physical sight—"between the sunlight and the shade"—and moves outward to a consideration of certain metaphysical sights. At the same time, Robinson involves the sense of hearing, of sound—sound and sight together. The poem begins with an autumnal scene, with the sight and the sound of leaves in the wind, and both figures will dominate the poem, as will the symbol of the leaves themselves, until by the last stanza we hear and see the leaves falling. The figure again belongs to that whole Robinsonian cluster of images that have to do with descent into darkness, of falling into the unknown, "where all who know may drown" as "The Man Against the Sky" concludes.

Throughout we find counterpointed both images and conceptualized renderings of hearing and seeing, of sound and sight, of darkness and light. The dominant image, however, is that of a tree, specifically, an oak. But I would not wish to give the impression that Robinson has written a Donnean Metaphysical set piece, wholly controlled by a single conceit or closely interlocked images, one developing out of another in immaculate order. The poem has too much weight of personal experience for a purely intellectual or fanciful substructure. And we know what Robinson thought of Donne's poetry, though it will not do to push a single statement in a letter to a doctrinaire conclusion. Nevertheless, everything we know of Robinson's life, tradition and imagination suggests strongly that the Metaphysical mode would not appeal to him. Hence in "Hillcrest" he follows a pattern we have seen many times in other short poems, that of a terse and spare line and idiom, firm rhymes; the lines are largely end-stopped, stanzas self-contained. Once Robinson has established the thematic and imagistic motifs of the poem, he is content to explore their intellectual, conceptualized implications, finally returning to the central cluster of images and ending the poem with a combination of statement and image.

The poem is about the equivocal nature of experience and wisdom. Both together make a man's life, yet they can hide themselves because man is an inattentive animal, always looking for ways to dodge the truth and to accept for real what merely pleases. In those rare interludes when a man withdraws from the stresses of ordinary living to take account of himself and his life, he may find himself contemplating not the victories he has, putatively, achieved, but defeats and errors. Such contemplation is not so hard to come by as it is to engage in deeply. It tells us far more than we want to know about what we have taken to be either our virtues or our defects. It can alter a man's view of himself and above all can force him to see that whatever injustices he may have felt, most of his hard luck is of his own making. And humility has the final word. If we tend to congratulate ourselves for our foresight, wisdom, endurance and insight; if we, equally, fall into self-pity, self-doubt, apprehension and intellectual obtuseness—why, this interlude between the seasons of summer and fall, between young manhood and middle age, "between the sunlight and the shade" can show us how small our victories have been, how deep the error runs, how fully we have in our pride deceived ourselves. But at the same time, the healing power of such contemplation can purge us of vanity and restore our courage, giving us the strength to see things as they are without flinching and to go on free of vanity and delusion.

Such a resumé leaves out the poem, of course; it commits the heresies of paraphrase and of interpretation concurrently, and the sin looms larger for being incomplete. I could analyze at length the ways in which Robinson can *imply* the imagistic motifs he first introduced while apparently talking in abstract terms. Indeed, I could at least suggest that the poem does indeed talk, has a conversational tone suggestive of "a man speaking to men." Such matters are important, yet insisted upon they may

kill the work—make it available as a corpse is available. Some
such methods have real usefulness for certain kinds of poetry,
and exegesis of some kind will always be necessary and good as
long as it disappears into all the other knowledge we have when
we really read poetry and don't just talk about it. The talk
that matters most, though, happens when we go beyond criticism
and exegesis and achieve that kind of "descanting" on "the
supreme theme of art and song," as Yeats has it.

At the end of "Hillcrest" the poet asks us to accept a world of
pain and uncertainty, without fear and without recrimination.
The close recalls Arnold's wistful desire "to see life steadily and
see it whole," but for Robinson the steadiness is all or nearly
such; to see it whole exceeds man's powers; the man who believes that he does see the whole becomes a "child who sees the
whole / World radiant with his own delight." Men have to
move and move outward, yet that motion must find a counterpart in the centripetal journey of the mind in search of meaning.
In this poem, Robinson is very precise in his categories and
descriptions. We have none of the vagueness of definition or
nomenclature found in such poems as "Octaves." Here he tells
us, in the context of a specific time, place, season and weather,
viewed literally and figuratively, just what it is that this contemplating man contemplates, while the sound of the wind in
the leaves bears the burden of "The roaring of a world remade /
And all his ruins and regrets." No cloudy transcendentals here;
only the hard experiences, the pettinesses and defeats that make
up life. In the face of such earned wisdom and humility as
this poem discloses without asserting, we can only give assent.
One of its great virtues depends on what it will not say, taking
the attitude that reticences sometimes speak more memorably
than rhetoric. Another and a determining virtue is the fine,
stoic irony that controls tone and feeling. An expression such as
"index of adagios" might sort well with a line by Hart Crane;
here it cuts with ironic edge into the human tendency to adorn
and falsify and to "tell it like it is." The only trouble with such
telling is that somehow, when one of those reality-mongers
starts to pass the word, it isn't like that at all, at all. Robinson
may in part be doing penance for pride in his own achievement, for presuming to tell the rest of humanity what's what.

At any rate, in the fine image of the oak trees of our own view of our achievement returning "to acorns out of which they grew" we have a witty, sardonic and imagistically satisfying epigram summing up the deluded vanity of the self-appointed reality-monger. What must count for a man as man and as poet is humility in the face of his smallness and ignorance, but with the courage to face these, smile at them, and go on.

One can always overdo it and claim too much for any poem. I might dwell with more profit, perhaps, on such a remarkable poem as "Eros Turannos" or on the complexities of "Mr. Flood's Party," or I might go to others less familiar but equally impressive. But enough is enough. I have done nothing by way of detailed analysis of any of the long poems because I think the job would be tedious in the case of most such works; were I to analyse "The Three Taverns," let us say, or "Rembrandt to Rembrandt," both blank verse monologues of middle length, I think I would risk substituting my analysis for a reader's reading. But most of all, I repeat that Robinson's poetry seems not to submit itself to the kind of analysis we have grown up with. Perhaps that, though it may have hindered his reputation, may in the long run have saved his poetry!

Robinson died on April 4th, 1935, shortly after two o'clock in the morning. From his room in New York Hospital where cancer patients who can afford it go to die, he had been able to see Welfare Island, and the comparison struck him forcibly. Hagedorn and Smith, who saw him in his last days and wrote about it, remark on his consideration for others, a trait that had always endeared and now seemed to many to have taken on another dimension. He received many visitors and worked away reading the proofs of *King Jasper,* a feat of attention one might have thought beyond him at that point. When he died, there was a group of friends at the hospital waiting for the end. When it came, 'as Auden wrote of Yeats, "he became his admirers." He passed as it were into legend and into that curiously jealous possession of those who have known a great poet. The MacDowell Colony preserved his memory, almost his presence, to an extent one might think oppressive, and no doubt the usual in-fighting took place among friends, acquaintances and putative lost ladies and lights-o'-love as to who had or could exercise eminent domain. We would all readily admit that a poet's friends and admirers need not be his best critics and biographers, but granted that close association and affection may affect disinterestedness, they nonetheless make possible certain views of and insights into the man if not the poet. It is up to those who never knew the man to try to know the poet so well that they can combine with the poetry reminiscences of the man, chiefly to help mere readers to see more in the poetry. Above all, readers want to feel that the poems came out of a man who lived, who, again like Auden's Yeats, was "silly like us." In Robinson's case we have to conclude that whatever the shortcomings of the man and the poet may have been, the man was a remarkable human being and the poet some kind of hero.

Robinson's attitude never assumed the heroic. Sardonic, diffident, ironic, sly, he sets before us in his better work images or patterns of human life and of events drawn from memory which have their power no less "to chasten and subdue," as Wordsworth says, than to instill in us "thought[s] / Of kindness and of love." He wrote out of sympathy for humanity to a large extent; people are at the heart of his best poetry, some nameless but many with names that have become permanent as such things go. Robinson wrote a poetry that moved between the two worlds of aesthetic absolutes on the one hand and realistic-sentimental plainsong on the other. As might be expected, neither camp welcomed him, and it has only been recently that numbers of the intellectually respectable have found it possible to like the poetry. In part the decline of the reputations of Eliot and Pound, the cultivation of informality, the casualness and Americanism of the present have been responsible. Robinson would care no more for the latter camp than he did for the former. If one of the defects of his poetry derives from a certain narrowness of view, the concomitant virtue shines clearer today than yesterday: what he saw, he saw steadily, and he did not go off whoring after strange whores—or gods. Again we have recourse to Kipling and his "gods of the copybook headings." Because he never became infatuated with novelty nor with experimentation apart from the thing he experimented with, he did not become merely decadent or "camp." Because he never really changed style or subject, he could work his narrower vein deeply. Yeats, who died soon after Robinson, shows us Robinson's true counterpart as man and poet. He had it made from the start, so to speak, and stands above all other moderns as the chameleon poet, the visionary, the rhetorician of a new rhetoric, the mythmaker and mystagogue. And as his wife told him, he was no saint. He turned his back on the "real" world and his "real" self to remake both closer to his heart's desire: ". . . man made up the whole / Lock stock and barrel / Out of his bitter soul."

How should an old-line Yankee like Robinson view such foreign goings-on? Though Robinson must have met John Butler Yeats, the poet's father, in the early Village days, it does not appear that he and the son ever met, nor can we imagine either having much sympathy for the other's poetics. They belong to different civilizations as well as races. We who have neither their passion nor their times in our veins can appreciate both. Where Robinson satisfies us as Yeats never can is in the claustrophobic vision of our desperate lives, all in some way redeemed by irony and sympathy and the promise that all this suffering and error is not in vain. Whether or not we ever read poetry for this kind of thing, we will get it from a poetry like Robinson's whether we know and like it or not, just as we will get from reading Yeats at his best a kind of exaltation on seeing man transcending himself. In a time when an intolerable deal of nonsense about creativity and living dangerously gets thrown around, one needs to get down to a few facts. Robinson and Yeats, almost exact contemporaries, serve to lay out the extreme boundaries of what we can call the Modernist Movement. When all the confusion has cleared, it may be seen that both poets set the terms and lay the groundwork. Realism. Romanticism. Humanism. Symbolism. At the hither extreme of the realist-humanist, Robinson's poetry begins; at the thither, Yeats's. Both meet in that middle ground, or better, element, where, Melville tells us, God takes his way.

Sidney and Shelley among others stress that poetry by its very nature teaches and gives pleasure; Coleridge insists on the latter. Today there is a tendency to forget that element, to think of poetry as good for you, full of cultural vitamins and minerals. Of course most art bores and irritates because most art is bad. How much survives from any age or period? But take away from the poet his power to please and his intent to instruct and you have disaster.

> When all the world would have a matter hid,
>   Since Truth is seldom friend to any crowd,
> Men write in fable, as old Aesop did,
>   Jesting at that which none will name aloud.
> And this they needs must do, or it will fall
> Unless they please they are not heard at all.

Thus Kipling—one of Robinson's favorites, remember—in "The Fabulists." Can men find real pleasure in the exercise of mind and imagination? Do they ever associate learning with delight? Can they feel joy in an image for its own sake? Robinson the analogist, the seeker for unillusioned "light," is a fabulist. The characters he invented or transfigured in his poems, the best of them, have exemplary functions—we have seen them performing. The pleasure a man takes defines his capacity to learn, and learning can be the greatest pleasure life affords. A poetry that does not teach cannot exist. But it teaches most truly by example, all unconscious, as art, of its own intent. Robinson knew himself to have been born one of those whose job it was to make those pleasurable instructional devices called poems. He did not plan to take delight in the circumstances surrounding the job. He did not expect a large audience, as no poet can. He felt that his poems could give delight and a sort of insight that no other contrivance could, and so, like Eben Flood, "knowing that most things break," he got to work. The time may be at hand when no true poetry can get a hearing—there have been and will be again such times:

> So it hath fallen, as it was bound to fall.
> We are not, nor we were not, heard at all.

Robinson was an old-line Yankee. Born between social and economic, as well as familial, worlds, he grew up in a time and in a society of rampant materialism, in which a person who would not engage in the commercial enterprise, had no financial resources and could not live by writing, must starve. Starve he did—in more ways than one. I think Yeats would have understood that kind of nobility. But Robinson was alone in his art as European writers have almost never been and as American writers, and those the best, have nearly always been. The life of poetry in America has usually had hardship to offer, and the effect, as we have seen, does damage. Yet the matter is temperamental too: Robinson might have played the game; he simply, for whatever reason, never did. Melville and Melville's Bartleby would have understood; "I would prefer not to," as the scrivener so irritatingly observed to his masters. Similarly Robinson, like Bartleby, never cried "No in thunder" because he did not see himself as either God or Satan but as "born on this isthmus of a middle state." He would laugh at the notion of the Artist as Culture Hero, or at the pretentiousness of so many writers and their claims to spiritual dangers and risks beyond mortal ken. He chose the middle style not because he could not fly high but because he knew that starting high means that one has nowhere to go but down, a not-infrequent occurrence with the apocalyptic and prophetic schools. Which is by no means to say that he does not descend to pedestrianism and worse. What often redeems a flawed poem and ensures a sound one is his awareness of other people and his Wordsworthian conviction that the poet was only a man like other men, but in a particular way, more so. The more so is what counts.

Selected Bibliography

"Selected" means what it says. For example, I include only books or monographs of some length, no notes and queries or essays. I have omitted books which seem to me to have been superseded by newer work and others which to me seem superfluous or merely wrong-headed. As I indicate in the text, much Robinson scholarship strikes me as second-rate, as most literary scholarship is bound to be. There is no one book on Robinson which combines all the many elements that make up a first-rate biographical and critical study. Nevertheless, the books listed below all seem to me to have considerable value.

As to the volumes of Robinson letters, I mention only two because although there are others they do not shed much light on the man or his work. In the next few years, one hopes, many of the letters and other pertinent documents will be released for publication.

As to editions of books of poems, the important information is to be found in the Hogan and Lippincott bibliographies. I list here only the editions of poems now in print. If the picture is not a very satisfactory one, all we can do is hope for a really first-class *Complete Poems,* preferably in two or three manageable volumes.

Books of Poetry

Collected Poems of Edwin Arlington Robinson. Macmillan, New York, 1937.

Selected Poems (edited by Morton Dauwen Zabel, with an introduction by James Dickey). Macmillan, New York, 1965.

Selected Early Poems and Letters of E. A. Robinson (edited by Charles T. Davis). Holt, New York, 1960.

Letters

Sutcliffe, Denham (ed.): *Untriangulated Stars: Letters to Harry de Forest Smith, 1890–1905.* Harvard University Press, Cambridge, 1947.

Torrence, Ridgely (ed.): *Selected Letters of Edwin Arlington Robinson.* Macmillan, New York, 1940.

Criticism and Biography

Barnard, Ellsworth: *Edwin Arlington Robinson.* Macmillan, New York, 1952.

Coffin, Robert P. Tristram.: *New Poetry of New England: Frost and Robinson.* Johns Hopkins Press, Baltimore, 1938.

Coxe, Louis O.: *Edwin Arlington Robinson.* University of Minnesota Press, Minneapolis, 1962.

Fussell, Edwin S.: *Edwin Arlington Robinson: The Literary Background of a Traditional Poet.* University of California Press, Berkeley, 1954.

Hagedorn, Hermann: *Edwin Arlington Robinson.* Macmillan, New York, 1938.

Neff, Emery E.: *Edwin Arlington Robinson.* Sloane, New York, 1948.

Robinson, W. R.: *Edwin Arlington Robinson: A Poetry of the Act.* Western Reserve University Press, Cleveland, 1967.

Smith, Chard Powers: *Where the Light Falls: A Portrait of Edwin Arlington Robinson.* Macmillan, New York, 1965.

Winters, Yvor: *Edwin Arlington Robinson.* New Directions, Norfolk, Conn., 1946.

Bibliography

Hogan, Charles Beecher: *A Bibliography of Edwin Arlington Robinson.* Yale University Press, New Haven, 1936.

Lippincott, Lillian: *A Bibliography of the Writings and Criticisms of Edwin Arlington Robinson.* Faxon, Boston, 1937.

Index